Aniisu has always been an evangelist for
indeed, he came to my attention 10 y
first commentator on internal commu
then, I have been delighted to publish his articles to a worldwide audience of thousands of practitioners on our website. His book will be a valuable cornerstone to anyone hoping to develop their career or just become a better communicator in the workplace.

Marc Wright
Chairman, simplygroup

In today's distributed workplace, internal communications (ICs) is the glue which holds the organization together. This book is a testimony to Aniisu's passion to spread the glue. Readers will walk away with a clear thought that IC is a strategic imperative for a successful execution of the company strategy. As the title of the book suggests, it not only shares choice of practices and models, it follows up with insights coming from real-life examples. Enjoy the book, and make sure you implement it in your workplace to enjoy the results!

Karandeep Singh
CFO, Flipkart and former
Managing Director,
Sapient in India

How do you put order in the world? The simplest and the most efficient way to do so is by putting one's own house in order! And the world around us, automatically and most often, is seen to be orderly! Internal communications is another way of putting order in one's own house—by managing the communications flow, devising efficacious communications strategies, and see to its effective implementation. Aniisu Verghese's book *Internal Communications:*

Insights, Practices, and Models, is a timely help to all of us—employers and employees, practitioners and academician alike. In it, he introduces and discusses a relatively new field of learning and relating in Indian corporate communications situations; the practice has always existed as a grossly neglected area, though. The book demonstrates its importance, and suggests a number of practical ways one can gainfully employ in any circumstance.

Father Richard Rego
Professor, St Aloysius
College, Mangalore
Station Director, SARANG
107.8F

Internal Communications: Insights, Practices, and Models is a veritable bible for practitioners in internal communications. It covers a gamut of essential topics in a crisp and succinct style. The lack of incorporating measurement yardsticks into the communications plan is what often prevents otherwise excellent entries from Asia from bagging awards at international competitions. Aniisu Verghese has addressed this and related issues by discussing the mandated need for communications audit, employee engagement and integrating social media into the internal communicator's job. Professionals following Verghese's leads, embellished with fascinating case studies, may well be equipping themselves to ultimately break the corporate glass ceiling and make themselves eligible for the board room. A sobering thought indeed!

Bish Mukherjee ABC
President, Misha Network
Sydney/Chennai

One of my earliest encounters with the internal communications practice was in 1996 during my stint with CITIL (Citicorp Information Technology Industries Limited), which later became i-flex solutions. We borrowed a maxim from our major shareholder, Citibank, which read 'if you feel good, you work good'.

Since then, things have changed rather dramatically. From being a poster in the corridor and an attractive in-house newsletter to a 'nice-to-have discussion' in the conference room, it has now become the lifeblood that flows through the veins of every organization. It has become the heartbeat of a company. And it continues to be so—behind the scenes.

Internal communications has finally got its recognition. Aniisu Verghese, through his book *Internal Communications: Insights, Practices, and Models* has done the profession great service by aggregating information and case studies through his tireless research and rich work experience. He has filled the big gap by clearly articulating the rigours of a profession that often receives paid lip service.

I am sure that *Internal Communications: Insights, Practices, and Models* will be the much needed inspiration for CEOs, professional communicators, and students alike who could use these learnings to enrich employee engagement that would ultimately lead to healthier performance and profits.

Peter Yorke
CEO, Yorke
Communications

Internal communications has had very blurred definitions until the early 1990s, and slowly corporates have warmed up to the idea that the bottom line does get affected by positive employee communications that lead to employee engagement and, thus, reducing attrition and hiring costs.

Aniisu K. Verghese has been instrumental in forming structures and formats for the vast realm that is communications and through this book explains the building blocks of internal communications resulting in engaged employees at work.

Anney Unnikrishnan
Head Corporate Communications
Allianz Trivandrum

INTERNAL
COMMUNICATIONS

INTERNAL COMMUNICATIONS

Insights, Practices, and Models

ANIISU K. VERGHESE

www.sagepublications.com

Los Angeles • London • New Delhi • Singapore • Washington DC

First published in 2012 by

SAGE Response
B1/I-1 Mohan Cooperative Industrial Area
Mathura Road, New Delhi 110 044, India

SAGE Publications Inc
2455 Teller Road
Thousand Oaks, California 91320, USA

SAGE Publications Ltd
1 Oliver's Yard, 55 City Road
London EC1Y 1SP, United Kingdom

SAGE Publications Asia-Pacific Pte Ltd
33 Pekin Street
#02-01 Far East Square
Singapore 048763

Published by Vivek Mehra for SAGE Publications India Pvt Ltd, typeset in 11/15 AGaramond by Tantla Composition Pvt Ltd, Chandigarh and printed at De-Unique, New Delhi.

Library of Congress Cataloging-in-Publication Data Available

ISBN: 978-81-321-0966-2 (PB)

The SAGE Team: Sachin Sharma, Puja Narula Nagpal and Anju Saxena

To my father, late Mr E. John Koshy—thank you for teaching me to value what life offers.

Thank you for choosing a SAGE product! If you have any comment,
observation or feedback, I would like to personally hear from you.
Please write to me at contactceo@sagepub.in

—Vivek Mehra, Managing Director and CEO,
SAGE Publications India Pvt Ltd, New Delhi

Bulk Sales

SAGE India offers special discounts for purchase of books in bulk.
We also make available special imprints and excerpts from our
books on demand.

For orders and enquiries, write to us at

Marketing Department
SAGE Publications India Pvt Ltd
B1/I-1, Mohan Cooperative Industrial Area
Mathura Road, Post Bag 7
New Delhi 110044, India
E-mail us at marketing@sagepub.in

Get to know more about SAGE, be invited to SAGE events, get on
our mailing list. Write today to marketing@sagepub.in

This book is also available as an e-book.

Contents

List of Illustrations

TABLES

FIGURES

Foreword

A s I write these lines on a breezy Trivandrum night in
Kerala, cooled by mountain breezes of the nearby Western
Ghats, I am completing a month-long Internal Communications
engagement that I began for a Fortune 500 company based out of
Seattle, USA. Many of those life-lessons in communication came
alive for me when I read Aniisu's book.

For months in the USA, I had access to the 'C-Suite', the
workspace of intense men and women who run global corporations.
And upfront, I saw them ask this question: 'How do we keep our
people in our organization informed, involved and inspired, in
order to achieve our corporate goals?'

Aniisu K. Verghese has the answer for you in his book *Internal
Communications: Insights, Practices, and Models*.

The greatest organizations, the iconic ones we admire from our
age, are built by men and women whose lives are transformed by
inspiring corporate visions. Internal Communications shape those
conversations which, in turn, create those great organizations.
So, wherever you are on our planet—North America, Asia
Pacific, Europe or an idyllic corner of Oceania—the principles of
communication, you will discover, are exactly the same.

Though we both live and practise our crafts as communicators in
sunny India, I first met Aniisu at an Internal Communicators online
forum based out of the UK. At this forum, Aniisu and I discovered

our common interest in the Holy Grail of Communicators the world over: Internal Communications.

Aniisu is a pioneering internal communicator, whose insights have enriched the communication world since 2006. He has a unique insight into the realm of Internal Communications. His Intraskope blog is home to some of the best insights in Internal Communications you will find across the World Wide Web.

Having worked in the communication space since 1990, I have yet to come across anyone with Aniisu's passion for Internal Communications. He takes every opportunity he gets to share what he has discovered about Internal Communications—as teacher, as blogger, and as industry speaker. Attending Aniisu's workshop 'Internal Communications 101 Workshop' at Bangalore in 2011 was the centre of the Internal Communications world. Professionals converged from every corner of India to have conversations around Internal Communications and to discover for themselves a rich lode of industry insight!

The value, for me, in Internal Communications 101 Workshop lay in its ability to meld research, insight, and theory into one vibrant learning experience. The practical exercises simulated real-life work environments. And for every participant, there were rich communication takeaways. *Internal Communications: Insights, Practices, and Models* will do the same for you.

Now that Aniisu's insights on Internal Communications have found their way into this book, it will change the way Internal Communicators think and strategize around their chosen craft. As an intrepid explorer on the horizons of Internal Communications, Aniisu opens new worlds of understanding for us. I personally look ahead to the new learning spaces this book will create for communicators worldwide.

So, whether you are taking your first steps or creating your internal communications niche, I recommend Aniisu's book to you. Read it. For it holds the keys to the kingdom of Internal Communications.

Joseph Fernandez
Author
Corporate Communications: A 21st Century Primer
Trivandrum, July 2012

Preface

The genesis of this book goes back to when I began my career in internal communications. I made numerous attempts to understand the function, researched it on the Internet, and talked to leaders. However, I found limited knowledge of the subject, especially in India. Practitioners relied on a few professionals who shared internal information or made an attempt to collaborate on topics of interest.

As I began learning the ropes and conceptualized, designed, and implemented various internal communications programmes, they shaped my thinking and germinated the need for a simple book that would explain what internal communications is and the way in which it works to improve how an organization conducts itself and engages its workforce.

In my interactions with students at various teaching assignments, I have often been asked by many on the possible ways to get a break in internal communications. Also, many corporate communicators have written to me seeking opportunities in this evolving function.

Rigour and Discipline

To me internal communications is about the fundamentals and rigour, a rigour that evokes a favourable response from staff and leaders. It is a systematic effort to align everyone on the same page, and drive change and behaviour. Just like how the professionalism and discipline of musicians create a symphony, internal communications builds pattern and predictability in an organizational set-up which reassures employees, guides leadership, and maximizes the potential of all stakeholders. Therefore, I included these elements in the title of the book, which highlights essentials for success and organizational certainty.

Understanding internal communications and making a mark take time. You need to be constantly upgrading your knowledge and learning more about trends. That is what the book helps uncover.

This book is an attempt to give internal communications the spotlight it deserves in organizations. Especially in India, the function has got limited attention and, therefore, most organizations hardly have teams dedicated to internal communications.

In this book, I attempt showcasing how internal communications practices can effectively deliver business results through practical models, strategies, and policies. It hopes to give a deep understanding of the key issues confronting the internal communications discipline today in India and abroad.

As a practitioner I believe this book will benefit any communications or human resources professional who would like to explore this critical function, apart from Media and Communications students looking at making a niche in this domain. I am hopeful this will be also a valuable resource for faculty in business management or communications schools.

Last, but not in the least, the book's emphasis is on creating increased awareness of the role internal communications plays in today's dynamic world. Among the perspectives you will gain are ways to raise the profile of internal communications within your organization, essential skills for internal communicators, and a review of challenges and benefits of integrating social media.

How to Best Use This Book

This book is designed keeping in mind the needs of professionals, students, and faculty as they go about their work, study, or teaching assignments. It will be beneficial also for non-profit organizations and public enterprises. It considers the shorter attention spans of readers and, therefore, you will notice short chapters with sections on insights, perspectives, and case studies that you can attempt based on concepts discussed.

The chapters follow a logical sequence—from starting out in internal communications, the fundamentals of the function, and gradually moves on to topics of relevance today—social media, leadership communications, measurement, and messaging among others.

If you are an internal communications professional, I encourage you to use material to think through your standing in your team and as a leader, have conversations at your team meetings, or have your team reflect on a chapter and present back to the group.

You can refer to the interviewing techniques and questionnaire while identifying talent. You are welcome to visit my blog Intraskope (www.intraskope.wordpress.com) and share perspectives on any of the chapters so that other readers can benefit from your point of view.

If you are a corporate communications faculty at an undergraduate or a B-school, this book can be used as a reference while teaching key concepts and elements of career planning in communications.

If you are a student, I request that you take the time to read each chapter in detail and refer to my blog for additional thoughts. Please remember that this is a high-level overview based on my experience and research reports that I have perused.

I am interested in your point of view as you browse this book. Do feel free to mail me directly at intraskope@yahoo.com

Acknowledgements

This book has been a journey to bring internal communications to the fore. Although it took me a while to crystallize my thoughts and put them in a format which will be relevant to students, practitioners, and communicators, I believe the journey has only begun.

There are many people who have contributed immensely to this book, and I want to acknowledge their insights, patience, and advice.

- My parents, for giving me a solid foundation despite limited resources and believing in my abilities to give back to this world in more ways than one.
- My wife Wilmmaa—the anchor of my life—for her selfless support in helping me find the 'mind space' to write this book. I couldn't have crossed the finishing line without her positive spirit. Our son Aadvay who gives us strength every day. I know how blessed I am to have you both in my life.
- Thanks to my students at St Joseph's College of Business Administration, Bangalore, and St Aloysius College, Mangalore, whom I taught and learnt immensely from during by stints as a visiting faculty. Your discerning viewpoints helped me along my journey to be a better professional and person.

- Father Richard Rego of St. Aloysius College—Professor and Station Director of SARANG 107.8FM who understands the power of communications, and in it being fundamental to professional and personal success.
- My colleagues and supervisors at the various organizations I worked with—thank you for the enriching interactions and experiences that shaped the thinking for this book. Two managers who deserve special mention—Peter Yorke, the former corporate communications leader at i-flex solutions (now Oracle Financial Services), and Mary Lass Stewart of Sapient Corporation. Peter for teaching me the fundamentals of communications and finding meaning at work; Mary Lass for giving me the latitude and encouragement to hone my strengths.
- Joseph Fernandez, the unassuming communications leader at UST Global and an acclaimed author, for seeding the thought of publishing a book on this subject and for selflessly mentoring me on the nuances of book publishing.
- Sachin Sharma—the affable editor, Puja Narula Nagpal for the editorial and production, and the team at SAGE Publications, India, for believing in the book's potential and for the rigour and fantastic turnaround time for getting things done right.

Last, but not the least, I thank God for protecting and guiding me as I continue my journey in His name.

CHAPTER 1

Understanding Internal Communications

Companies that communicate effectively are much more likely to report high levels of employee engagement versus firms that communicate less effectively. Internal communications—a field that actively engages and communicates with internal stakeholders (employees, leadership, contract staff, and alumni)—is growing rapidly. This chapter showcases how internal communications practices can effectively deliver business results through practical models, strategies, and policies.

In this chapter, I share what internal communications mean, expectations from the role, and what you must seek answers to before you begin your journey. You will learn perspectives on skills and capabilities that internal communicators need to make a difference to.

In 2001, an Indian software company began independently running operations after taking wing from its parent organization. Keen to integrate its 2,000 employees across the globe, the firm began exploring options to energize, connect, and empower their staff. After debating the many possibilities, the leadership team believed it made sense to revamp their existing intranet.

As an internal communications manager, I discovered through surveys and informal conversations that the intranet didn't appeal to employees. Staff found it boring and mostly used the intranet to dump content which they didn't need or manage to send via emails. The young staff (average age: 23) preferred a hip site with cool functionalities and services. To make matters worse, employees rarely visited the intranet since the information didn't match their expectations.

I realized that a dramatic change in mindset meant getting all stakeholders including HR, business leaders, the CEO, project teams, learning, and development aligned as well as involving staff in designing the new-look intranet. To make the intranet appeal, we reorganized content keeping in mind business expectations, knowledge sharing, and special interest groups. For example, the business space covered subjects such as company update, a 'know your leader' column, CEO's message, and business performance; the knowledge sharing forum included discussions, polls, project problem solving, while the creative space included hobbies and interests that encouraged interaction and learning. We collated key employee tasks on the intranet to make it the only gateway into the organization. The emphasis on autonomy for office content by respective content stewards enabled faster updates to the intranet. We took the plan to senior management and got their buy-in and support to promote the 'new destination' for employees.

It didn't end there. Launching, marketing, and promoting the intranet featured among the most critical parts of this large-scale company-wide internal communications and change management exercise. The intranet got rebranded and we enrolled intranet content champions, conducted road shows, created a demo video, and showcased pages which got the most activity. We had leaders dive into the intranet and participate in discussions.

In a post-launch survey conducted to gauge impact, we received an overwhelming thumbs up for the intranet. We also received a large number of employee content contributions. Overall, the organization calculated a sizable return on investment for the intranet within a short span of the launch.

Taking Aim with Internal Communications

The above-mentioned case—see 'Intranet by the People, for the People' (Koshy and Yorke, 2002)—showcases one example of how and when internal communications works.

If you look closely at the case, it has key themes and fundamental elements running through, which are as follows:

Alignment: Understanding the issue and *getting everyone on the same page* for organizational momentum.

Inclusiveness: Thinking of an effective solution and *involving all stakeholders* for a sustainable and consistent experience.

Measurement: *Learning from metrics* and looping feedback to improve internal communications.

In this book, I will be referring to them as AIM as an acronym and as a simple reference point when we discuss cases. I refer to them as the essentials for any internal communications programme. There will be a few cases that we will refer to and try this framework as we progress in this book. I will call it a Workshop—so that it will be easy for readers to see how the situation can be solved by applying these principles.

According to the Watson Wyatt Communication Return on Investment (ROI) Study (Watson Wyatt, 2005), a significant improvement in communications effectiveness is associated with a nearly 20 per cent increase in a company's market value. Also, companies that communicate effectively are 4.5 times more likely to report high levels of employee engagement versus firms that communicate less effectively. To relaunch an intranet, the internal communications team didn't merely put a plan and kick-off, it needed to get 'buy-in' and all stakeholders on the same page. The team made a business case and demonstrated how the intranet will transform the way the organization works in the future. That vision needed the full support of the senior leaders as well as those who were going to get impacted. Keeping the community and stakeholders on the same page helps to improve adoption and the success rate of any roll-out.

The relaunch of the intranet depended heavily on how employees engaged at the start. Therefore, the team's attempt to involve employees early played out to their advantage. They were given ownership of pages and content, they were involved in the promotion, and also recognized for their support. According to the Communications Consultancy CHA Study (Melcrum, 2005), workers who know what the company plan is, are five times more likely to be motivated.

The intranet's launch comprised one part of the measurement, and it plays an important part in the success of any internal communications. A Melcrum (2004) report indicated that 66 per cent of internal communications practitioners surveyed didn't have a measurement strategy in place and did not consider a connection between communications performance and business goals. Research studies have indicated that improvements in communications programmes that drive supervisor or manager behaviour increased the market value of the firm by an average of 7.3 per cent (English, 2005).

Internal communications, a field that actively engages and communicates with internal stakeholders (employees, leadership, contract staff, and alumni), is growing rapidly. Several research reports and trends point to internal communications as being among the fastest growing areas of communications, although researchers admit that is a fairly new area and not top of mind in theory or practice.

A global study (Internal Communications Hub, 2009) commissioned by HSBC in partnership with UffindellWest, a brand and communications consultancy, reveals the outcomes of internal communications as relating to themes such as creating understanding of strategy and direction, supporting change management, information employees, building pride, and enabling connection to the company values.

Defining Internal Communications

Internal communications has been defined by researchers in multiple ways—to signify the relation with stakeholders, the process, or the approach. Two researchers, Welch and Jackson (2007), from the UK defined internal communications as the 'strategic management of interactions and relationships between stakeholders at all levels within organizations across a number of interrelated dimensions including internal line management communications, internal team peer communication, internal project peer communication and internal corporate communication'. Their approach broadens existing literature on internal communications, although the researchers highlight the need for empirical study to ascertain the concept's strength.

Other stakeholders include strategic management, day-to-day management, work teams, and project teams such as internal communications group. Internal communications, according to them, is designed to improve organizational commitment and build a sense of belonging among employees.

Hanna Kalla (2005) discussed how integrated internal communications is more representative of the domain and defined it as 'all formal and informal communications taking place in an organization'.

Internal communications is known to work in partnership with HR, either as a division with the group, within Marketing, or as a separate entity that reports into the CEO's office.

The practice of internal communications has transformed from a traditional domain to that which embraces technology and deals with staff as consumers. The focus today has shifted to building relationships and motivating employees became central to how management viewed their people.

The Case for Internal Communications

There is consensus on the value and importance of internal communications.

Organizations that invest in internal communications stand apart from the rest and have engaged staff. Considering how educated employees are today, they seek information on their own and are looking at organizations that can help clarify questions (Internal Communications Hub, 2008).

Internal communications is known to influence information sharing and knowledge transfer, impact change management, improve relationship building, and allow for two-way communication. Companies which communicate effectively have been able to increase their market value (Solari, 2012).

The commonly accepted roles of the internal communications function are to develop atmosphere of respect, employee commitment, belonging, unified identity, buy-in involvement, and engagement in support of the achievement of business goals. Employees who are committed to the organization, identify personally with it, are concerned about its future and are loyal to it will pursue its success.

Likewise, the benefits of internal communications include identification, motivation for a common cause, and managing change.

Growing Interest in Internal Communications

According to the 2003/2004 Watson Wyatt Communication ROI Study™ (Watson Wyatt, 2004), timing and type of communication can influence behaviour change and generate ROI for the organization.

In a later study by the same organization—the Watson Wyatt 2009/2010 Communication RO I Study™ (Towers Watson, 2010)—they discovered that among the 42 per cent of companies surveyed, the communication function played a strategic role in decision-making.

The Corporate Leadership Council (2004) states that among the top 25 drivers of engagement, employees' connection to the organization and internal communications ranks in the top five.

Today there is more emphasis on internal communications with it getting closely aligned to corporate strategies. Also, companies are funding programmes a lot more and communicators are seen as strategic consultants.

The Insidedge Employee Communications Best Practices Study (Insidedge, 2006) indicates that among the notable shifts, internal communications is seen to have moved from a state of 'passing information' to that of influencing behaviour and improving the organization's success rates.

In a global study conducted by the International Association of Business Communicators (IABC) Research Foundation (2005) to understand best practices in meeting the top employee communication challenges of the 21st century, what emerged is the importance of communication to support employees to connect to the strategy, educate and engage leaders, reduce information overload, and measure.

Internal communications professionals are often misunderstood as the 'poor' cousins of the recognized 'public relation' executives. However, in recent times that has changed. Today's internal communicator is seen as a corporate information strategist and plays a vital role in reinventing organizations. Internal communications as a subject is sparsely understood by practitioners, academics, and students alike due to difficulty in accessing internal information; limited research in this field; and a lack of emphasis on this domain as compared to other marketing communication functions.

Understanding the Role

So what are you expected to do when you sign up? Here are some of my recommendations.

If you are still in college I would recommend that you focus on one of the fastest-growing corporate communications functions— internal communications. It will drive how organizations continue to build internal equity and keep their staff engaged. There isn't a more powerful function than internal communications which can shape how leaders view their workforce and employees can interact on a common platform.

I encourage internal communicators to research the organization, the function, and the leader either through sources in the industry or from the Internet.

Visit the company's website and understand more about what the organization does and how it articulates it vision.

Take time to imbibe the company's values and culture.

As a new hire, you will be oriented on the organization's business and goals. Make it a point to not just clarify your doubts but to also observe how the induction process works and in which way you can improve it.

Remember you have a fresh outlook and have hopefully an unbiased view of the first crucial employee connection. You may be called in to articulate how the new-hire orientation can be transformed. As an internal communicator, the employee value proposition is as important to deliver as a message at the early stage of an employee's journey. So if you aren't getting a great experience, ensure to make a note and think through a better way of running it.

THE FIRST FEW WEEKS

In the first few weeks of joining the internal communications group, you may be asked to meet and greet internal stakeholders and familiarize yourself with how the team functions. This may include travelling to other sites or locations where a majority of employees are based or where leaders sit.

- You are expected to immerse yourself in the available literature and resources such as company brochures and the intranet to learn as much (and as quickly) as you possibly can.

- Ask specifically for recent research reports, internal studies on engagement, and survey conducted to gauge the impact of internal programmes.
- Read employees' comments. If you are hired at a middle or senior management level, the 'hit the road' call will come sooner.
- Keep a note of questions that niggle and ensure you ask them when you connect with your supervisor.
- Also, keep track of your conversations with stakeholders and document as much of the expectations as they have of you.
- Keenly observe interactions by leaders and understand the dynamics of the workplace.
- Set up a daily or a weekly checkpoint with your supervisor to know what is expected from you in the immediate future and what you can consider as part of your overall role.
- Maintain a list of all the work you do however transactional they may sound.
- Seek out tenured leaders and communicators and seek inputs on what will make one successful at the workplace.
- Ask your teammate if you can shadow them at work so that you get a better sense of the expectations.
- Lastly, if you find you do not have enough work to keep you occupied, seek it out!

For questions you should attempt getting answers to, look up 'Guide to Getting Answers When You Begin' *in the Resources section.*

After over a decade in internal communications I believe there are a few critical success factors for a professional to make a mark in this function, which include the following:

- The maturity of the organization to understand the power of internal communications.
- The open culture within the function and in the organization.
- Leadership commitment and support.
- Resources and tools to be successful as an internal communicator.

While the above-mentioned factors are vital, according to me, the quality of internal communications is directly related to the internal communicator's maturity and drive.

WORKSHOP

Let us examine the three-part AIM framework and see how it works in a situation.

Situation: Your office administration team is planning a Fire Prevention Week to get staff aware of the impact of fires in the workplace. In the recent past, there have been numerous such workplace fires and especially in high-rise complexes the rates of accidents and deaths from burns have spiralled. However, for busy professionals this topic is rarely top of mind and the team is struggling to get staff to keep this topic on their radar. They approach your internal communications team with a set of posters and other mailers that they intend communicating with. How will you refer to the three-part framework so that the team gets the best outcome from their campaign?

Intervention

Before you begin, what can be potential questions you can ask the team? Here are some examples:

- What is the purpose or what are the objectives of this campaign?
- How will you know if you are successful?
- What is the current mindset about fire prevention?
- What does research tell us about how people perceive such communication?

Alignment: *Getting Everyone on the Same Page* for Organizational Momentum

As part of the plan, the team can build a case for running this campaign as it will improve workplace safety, enhance staff's perceptions of the company ("I believe my organization is committed to my welfare", "I feel safe in my workplace", "I know my firm is interested in my safety"), and demonstrate potential savings from losses. This will appeal to the leadership team and key decision makers. The plan will need to be shared ahead of the roll-out so that there aren't any "surprises". It can include demos, drills, tours, and addresses by the local fire brigade apart from quizzes and other fun activities that focus on safety. Publish a calendar on your intranet so that all are aware of the schedule and can plan their work ahead. No one wants to be interrupted in the middle of a meeting with a fire drill!

Inclusiveness: *Involving All Stakeholders* for a Sustainable and Consistent Experience

Putting the plan in place is great but without all stakeholders pooling in ideas and playing a part, the event is heading for a stand-off. Seek suggestions for improvement of fire safety. Ask people to report any incidences they spotted in the recent past. Recognize staff that has made a difference to fire safety. Open up a hotline for sending in communication. Review previous surveys on workplace safety and incorporate recommendations—and let staff know that you considered it. Identify fire safety wardens and train the group. Provide them with resources so that they are known in the community.

Measurement: *Learning from Metrics* and Making Progress from Feedback

Gauge how the communication is perceived. Do a dipstick poll or run a survey to understand impact. Make tweaks to the campaign if you get feedback as you make progress. Report out the best practices and success stories from the campaign so that stakeholders know. Publish an article on the event on the intranet. Get your leaders to thank those who participated.

CASE STUDY

Rajesh runs Assertive Corp, a five-year-old medical transcription provider, with clients globally and a workforce of 5,000 employees spread across five Indian cities. He is keen to impress upon his board of directors to invest in an internal communications function that improves engagement and productivity. Over the past year he has seen increased attrition and reduced motivation levels. As an internal communications consultant, help craft a business case for Rajesh which he can present to his board.

Potential questions to frame your responses:

- What are the tangible outcomes of internal communications?
- How can he test the waters?
- What are the investments needed?
- Where can you find the right people?

STUDENT EXERCISE

Your college is launching an e-magazine for faculty, students, and prospective candidates. You are invited to support the development of the newsletter and propose recommendations for ensuring your audiences participate actively and contribute to content. What questions will you seek answers to before sharing your plan?

CHAPTER 2

Internal Communications Basics

The basics of internal communications involve effective planning, types of internal communications, and interventions that address short- and long-term issues.

In this chapter, I discuss the benefits of effective planning, the art and science of internal communications, and type of internal communications that organizations manage with.

The Open House Annual (OHA) at i-flex solutions (currently Oracle Financial Services Limited) is a forum to involve and keep its employees abreast of the company's progress and future plans. It encourages interaction between the senior management and staff, which serves as a platform for getting all employees on the same page. Celebrated across offices annually, it also serves as an occasion to recognize outstanding performances and efforts. Every year, employees are invited to join in the production of a theme video apart from participating in cultural events, showcasing the company's progress (Yorke, 2004). (Full disclosure: the author worked as Assistant Manager—Corporate Communications at i-flex solutions between 2000 and 2004 and directly contributed to the company's internal communications efforts and this event.)

Alignment: *Getting Everyone on the Same Page*

As the organization expanded across geographies, constantly motivating a young IT workforce was a challenging task. At that point in time, i-flex had 2,800 employees in 11 development centres, 20 overseas locations, and 3 subsidiaries. About 25 per cent of its employees worked overseas in about 40 countries. At least 600 employees joined every year. Traditional models of communication failed to build internal brand ambassadors. Most organizations rely on their physical environment to give employees a sense of well-being and identity.

Findings from an internal engagement study indicated the need for organizational clarity and alignment to goals. Better participation in corporate decisions, information sharing, work-life balance, freedom of self-management teams were among other asks. Notice how measurement plays a key role in considering the internal communications focus areas.

Inclusiveness: *Involving All Stakeholders*

The objectives were to execute a successful, unique campaign that raises awareness and builds internal brand ambassadors among employees, both domestic and international. All efforts were focused on encouraging employees to 'live' the brand and invest in the company.

Posters showing a 'smiling face' created from a collage of employees' photographs made staff feel part of the programme. Save-the-date mailers, intranet notes, and leadership messages got people excited. Employees across locations were included in a video that captured the vibrant corporate work culture. This video formed a critical element of the event and was used later as a sales collateral.

The event held at prominent venues in Bangalore and Mumbai comprised in-depth business presentations, interactive question and answer (Q&A) sessions, long service, team and excellence awards, and an employee-orchestrated entertainment session. The event was interspersed with customer and employee interviews apart from the popular i-flex 'human touch' and 'branding' audiovisuals.

MEASUREMENT: LEARNING FROM METRICS

Post-event, a page was created on the intranet with links showcasing the highlights of the show. Highlights were also concerted into a multimedia video and sent to all employees. The corporate newsletter also had a section dedicated to the event, with insights and interviews with key personnel. Employee communications outreaches called the 'overseas' OHAs were conducted with the help of local resources and senior management at individual locations abroad.

On the company and the technology fronts, many new employees were unaware of the company's progress in the market-place. This event succeeded in changing the perception by reinforcing the company's message as a global, technology-savvy leader with a human touch.

The post-event survey showed a marked increase in the awareness and satisfaction levels of the employees. Employee attrition dropped and people found the intranet as a very reliable resource of information.

In the example given above, notice how **AIM** gets practised to empower, involve, and measure the success of the initiative.

Internal Communications Analogies

Among the nine communication practices that are directly linked to an increase in shareholder, 'having a formal communication process in place' ranks among the top three that impacts ROI for an organization (Watson Wyatt, 2004). The Watson Wyatt ROI study spells out the importance of internal communications. The formal plan needs to include a documented communication strategy and implementation plan.

In simple terms, internal communications can be likened to the following analogies:

- The human body in which the heart controls the flow of blood through the network of veins and the brain which manages the information processing.
- A tree with its roots anchoring it to the earth and the branches forming the structure on which leaves and fruits grow.

- A river with tributaries fed constantly with unhindered flow of water.
- It is often referred to as the 'glue' which holds organizations together, an excellent metaphor describing the potential of internal communications.

Likewise, the internal communications oversees the planning and framework, crafting of messages, the flow of content, and influences the outcome for an organization.

The mathematical transmission model describes one among the earliest thoughts of communication involving information source, transmitter, channel, receiver, and destination (Shannon, 1948). They classified communication systems within which this model operates as discrete, continuous, and mixed. A discrete system is one in which both the message and the signal are a sequence of discrete symbols, for example, telegraphy. A continuous system is where the message and signal are both treated as continuous functions, for example, radio or television. A mixed system has both discrete and continuous variables appear, for example, transmission of speech. This model is widely followed as a base for developing theories on internal communications and measuring efficacy.

Building Blocks of Internal Communications

Internal communications is a subset of organizational or corporate communications, which also includes domains such as advertising, public relations, event management, marketing communications, and direct marketing. It empowers employees to do their jobs to the best of their ability and ensure that all are aligned to the organization's goals.

Internal communications needs to be aligned to the organization's goals. It aims to support leadership in crafting suitable messages, managing communication channels, writing, organizing, editing, and reviewing content. It also coaches employees in understanding the organization's values, mission, their role and responsibilities, and promotes adoption of appropriate communication strategies. There are three pillars of internal communications: strategy and fundamentals, skills and capabilities, and presence and growth.

Strategy and fundamentals: This refers to the basic and advanced understanding that an internal communicator needs to have to make a difference at work. It refers to defining and getting immersed in the culture of the organization. It expects that the individual will have requisite knowledge of processes, channels, content, planning, messaging, engagement, writing, and editing. The internal communicator also must be a team player who can multitask at work.

Skills and capabilities: While the communicator gets to create communication at work, the need is also to have strong programme and change management skills while understanding the pulse of staff and basics of design and user interface.

Presence and growth: The third phase involves getting into implementing solutions and measuring outcomes. It is important to understand the timing and frequency of communication so as to avoid overwhelming or confusing your audience. Staying consistent with quality of output and keeping a firm grip on budgets are vital for the success of any communication. Communication needs to be backed by strong research studies that gauge the pulse of the organization and provide timely feedback on the effectiveness of communication. Measuring impact of communication, seeking and evaluating feedback, building a sense of community and assisting human resources and business groups to motivate and improve engagement among their employees are among other objectives of internal communications.

The organization's core values and guiding philosophies are to be the anchor for the internal communications approach and strategy.

Therefore, the building blocks of internal communications are as follows (given in Figure 2.1):

Figure 2.1   Internal Communications Framework

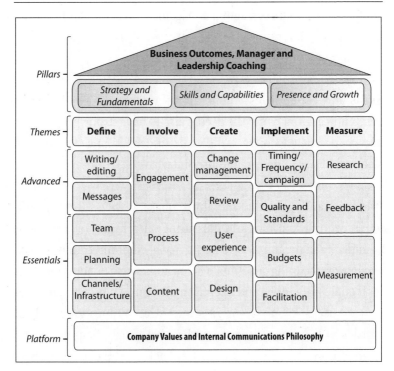

Source: Model proposed by the author.

Internal Communications Approaches

In my experience, I have observed three distinct types of internal communications:

- **Shoot and Scoot:** In this technique, you aim to cover all audiences and get out of the way. The impact of your communication can't be measured but there is a fair possibility of the messages reaching.
- **Pick and Tick:** In this scenario, the communicator is able to identify a few reasonable best 'bets' on getting the message through and looks at the communication as a one-off which gets off the list once the job is done.
- **Mine and Manage:** Here the communicator is a consultant and mines for insights that will deliver the maximum impact. The messages are targeted and thereafter managed to ensure feedback is considered and the next programme improved. There is a lot more focus to understand the audience.

Another way to approach internal communications is by balancing the push versus pull effects—which means you can publish communication top-down and also make it creative and interesting enough for staff to get excited in supporting the communication or even seeking information.

While the key features of good internal communications practices include timely, clear, concise, informative, and interesting, there are a myriad of challenges facing organizations today. Operating across different time zones, different regulations on communications, the varying quality of local communication channels, fractured employee audience profiles, the need to translate information into local language and context, corporate versus local centres, loyalty to functions and regions, and quality of communicators make up for a few critical challenges.

To further accentuate the situation, leading changes in the employment market are forcing organizations to rethink their strategies. Today, according to research, employees are not chasing 'careers for life', and the best 'top 10 per cent' decide to choose the organization rather than the other way around. What this means is decrease in workforce loyalty, attrition issues, and focus on reputation problems.

Therefore, there is a need to balance how much of communication can be administered, when the emphasis should be on listening and when it must be to inform and even more critical, what expectation can be accepted and what needs to be defined.

What Is a Typical Internal Communications Programme?

Just like the intranet relaunch programme, a typical communication programme roll-out will require planning, strategizing, budgeting, messaging, influencing, facilitating, measuring, and reporting. The programme might involve design and production of collateral, which can be managed in-house or outsourced depending on budgets and the need. It will expect the internal communicator to have a sound business understanding, leverage of an internal network of contacts, a good grasp of writing, and creativity and consulting skills.

It can range from the launch of a simple survey to a complex organization-wide intervention to improve morale or to ensure employees are aligned to a company objective. Therefore, the level of effort can vary from a day to many months.

The scope and scale of communication interventions are defined largely by the business environment and the organization's interest in employee engagement and communication. Most multinationals operating in India leverage the skills and

experience of professionals from their global network to introduce best practices in the region. Issues like attrition, stiff
competition for the limited talent pool (specifically in the IT
industry), and engagement are also drivers to champion internal
communications.

The basics of internal communications involve effective
planning. Planning begins with understanding the business
context, your audiences, the current challenges, the organization's
objectives, and interventions that address short- and long-term
solutions. (See Figure 2.2.)

Understanding the business context: Begin with scanning
the company's website, annual reports, leadership messages,
business updates, and the intranet's company news sections.
Know what the organization does, what are its differentiators, how
do clients perceive its offerings, how successful is the strategy,

Figure 2.2   Internal Communications Flow Chart

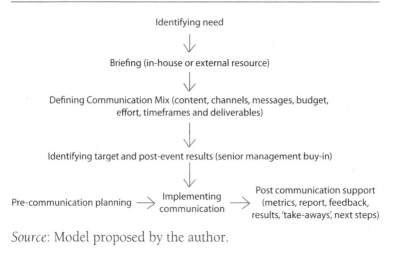

Source: Model proposed by the author.

what were the key milestones along its journey, and what lessons did the organization adopt. Also read media articles on the organization and which research agencies have reflected on its potential.

Your audiences: Seek employee engagement studies conducted in the organization, the recommended actions taken, and the outcomes. It is important to understand the different career levels, the average age of the groups, the perceptions employees have about the workplace, their aspirations and expectations. This is where getting a good sense of the employee life cycle enables constructive thinking.

Internal Communications Through the Employee Life Cycle Lens

Understanding the employee life cycle allows an internal communicator to gauge the range of communication that impacts the experience of the individual. It can be a 'hire-to-retire' model which looks at the on-boarding, learning, growth, maturity and exit phases, and the opportunities where internal communications interventions influence their understanding of the organization's goals.

Another way to slice the employee life cycle is to look at the contribution and value they add to the organization—I call it the 'value chain' model (see Table 2.1). The reason is that it considers the various aspects of the employee value proposition that organizations provide to staff. It considers the various stages an employee goes through with an organization and after exiting, and thinks through a structured approach to communication effectively.

Table 2.1 Internal Communications Value Chain Model

Stage	Pre-joining	Induction	Post-joining	Growth	Alumni
Communication Messages	Grow your career with us. You should consider an organization with potential and one which considers your growth as its priority.	You have made the right decision by joining us. Listen to our leaders, talk to peers, and know more about your role in our journey. Understand how you can develop yourself and contribute to the organization's success.	Get familiar with the culture, imbibe our values. Ask questions, seek mentors, and be relevant to your colleagues. Read up the intranet and know our policies and processes.	Set benchmarks, be approachable, and be a role model for others who join the organization. Set up others for success while owning your own growth. Seek opportunities to expand your knowledge and learning every day. Contribute building to our brand image in the marketplace.	We encourage you to stay connected with your alma mater. Keep us posted on opportunities to collaborate, refer people who may be a match for us, and consider joining us again when you believe there is an opportunity.

(Continued)

Stage	Pre-joining	Induction	Post-joining	Growth	Alumni
Communicator	Hiring lead, recruiter	CEO, business leads, HR leads	Supervisor, colleagues, business heads	HR, supervisor, peers	HR, business heads
Channels	Email, face-to-face interactions, connect forums, social media vehicles	Face-to-face sessions, email, video, leadership connect forums	Face-to-face conversations, email, intranet, community forums	Intranet, training, and mentoring forums	Alumni network, email, forums
Expected Impact	'I feel this organization offers me what others don't. I believe there is a career for me.'	'I think I made the right choice by joining here. I feel great to be in this organization. I know of the organization's plans and how I fit in.'	'I see how my career can evolve over time. I have the right people to support me in my journey. I am equipped with the right tools and resources.'	'I am excited by the growth in this place. I see myself as a mentor to others who join here. I feel like inviting others to join this firm.'	'I know I can always come back to my former firm. I have friends at my earlier workplace. I know I can consider a job opening later in my career.'

Source: Author.

Internal Communications Strategy and Planning

Before getting started, the role of the internal communicator is to define the strategy and plan for success.

An internal communications survey conducted by Karian and Box (2008) among HR and communication professionals across the UK found that only about 73 per cent say their organization had a communications plan.

There are downsides of not having a concrete plan or integrating resources. Lack of integration in communication leads to inefficiency and duplication and sometimes confusion about who and what an organization stands for.

What Should Your Strategy Document Contain?

- Start by defining the goals for the team and for the organization from a communication perspective—as in 'enable employees to be successful in their roles', 'leverage information and colleagues to solve problems', or 'improve their reach and credibility as business communicators'.
- Talk a bit about the philosophy at your organization—when it comes to communication. For example, do you expect it to be simple, direct, effective, personal, etc.
- In the next section, address your audiences and their current perceptions. Also how this strategy aims to overcome the issues.
- Then discuss how it impacts the choices people make with, say, channel selection or the impact on the ground with clients.
- Put a measure on the effectiveness and outcomes from internal communications.

My sense is that there will be two separate documents—one for internal to stakeholders and for your team, and the other meant for all people at the organization. This helps keep everyone on the same page. The former will give pointers on what stakeholders can expect from the team and the process and the latter can be more about how they can leverage the team's support and channels available.

In the next section, you may need to talk about the messages which need to be reinforced across the board—that communication is everyone's ownership, that among the leader's role is to also support their team's understanding of the strategy, etc.

It is important to talk about global trends in communications to reinforce how important internal communications is to the organization.

Put out clear goals on what you want to achieve. For example, 'based on our annual internal communications survey we expect 80 per cent employees to feel satisfied with the quality, accuracy and transparency of our communication' or 'leadership communication will see 70 per cent improvement in reach and credibility'.

Call out all support services and what your team can't do but can support/coach. Highlight your service-level agreements (SLAs).

Lastly, mention how and who employees and stakeholders can contact to have a discussion.

The internal communications planning includes the following steps:

- **Identifying business challenges:** Through literature and interviews with business stakeholders.
- **Reviewing audience perceptions:** By audits, focus group discussions, and surveys.
- **Defining objectives:** What do we want to aim for?

- **Arriving at outcomes:** Knowing what we can achieve and get positive results for.
- **Crafting suitable messages:** Articulating what we want our audiences to know or take action on.
- **Selecting the channels:** This varies based on the impact and reach you need. If your organization is geographically spread, then electronic channels or local leadership need to make contributions. If the information is critical and needs discussion, a face-to-face mode is preferred. The channel selection also varies by your audiences' preferences. For example, younger workforces, especially in India, prefer electronic channels while older staff expects face-to-face connections.
- **Know your communicators and content reviewers:** Preselect your communicators and get familiar with those who will review/approve the messages.
- **Measure impact:** Did we get to our audience, did they do what was expected, are we successful in our communication?
- **Budgeting:** Are you equipped to fund your campaign well? Do you have all the resources to make your campaign successful?

Touch versus Impact Internal Communications Model

I am proposing a model for internal communications which identifies the best use of time by communicators while delivering best practices.

From a stakeholder context, everyone expects the same level of support from the internal communications team. However keen you may be, you will need to prioritize and focus your attention to deliver the maximum impact with stakeholders.

Therefore, you need to ensure your energies and resources are directed at those who can make the most of internal communications.

Often I have been asked why does a certain leader get more attention over another? What determines who gets what focus?

To understand this, it helps to view this engagement through the lens of the internal communications team and the stakeholder's level of understanding.

A stakeholder is defined as one who needs the direct involvement and support for enabling change through internal communications. The stakeholder can be the senior management, business leads, team leaders, project teams, the HR department, the corporate social responsibility team, the crisis communication group, or the mergers and acquisitions manager.

The higher the level of understanding, the lower the level of support that is needed. However, to begin with, an internal communicator can begin in the low touch–low impact quadrant and move up the quadrants based on resources and stakeholders' understanding of the function.

I have articulated a 2 × 2 touch versus impact model.

LOW TOUCH–LOW IMPACT

This scenario can occur at an early stage of introducing internal communications interventions in an organization. The internal communicator has only limited resources at hand and can only manage to deliver low impact. For example, if there is a need to review a communication artefact as a tactical piece, the communicator is only able to have limited influence on the overall campaign.

HIGH TOUCH–LOW IMPACT

This scenario can occur when there is a skill deficiency in the company, for example, if stakeholders are unable to write lucidly or articulate their thoughts. In such cases, the internal communicator may invest time to coach; however, it may not lead to a great deal of change. The communicator may be exhausting time on hand in this case. Moreover, if stakeholders do not feel accountable for their communication, the communicator may find his team's effort in this quadrant. The ideal scenario is to move away from this quadrant into the 'low-touch–high-impact' zone.

HIGH TOUCH–HIGH IMPACT

In this quadrant, the internal communicator is aware of the effort in making a dramatic difference to the organization's goals with all hands on board. For example, if there is a large-scale change management exercise, then the communicator will need to draw the support of all team members to conceptualize, plan, execute, and measure outcomes for the campaign. This will mean some stakeholders will get limited support. The campaign will have the backing of, say, an executive sponsor, and the internal communicator will be involved right from the start. This however isn't a suitable position to be in, and setting the right expectations at the beginning will help the team's morale.

LOW TOUCH–HIGH IMPACT

The way to approach the communication support is via a build–operate–transfer model.

That means to say that the team must aim to be in the low-touch–high-impact box from high-touch–high-impact quadrant (see Figures 2.3 and 2.4).

Figure 2.3 Touch versus Impact Internal Communications Model: Basic

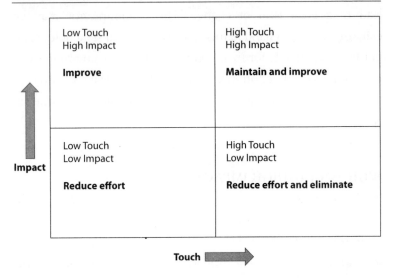

Source: Author.

Figure 2.4 Touch versus Impact Internal Communications Model: Best-case Scenario

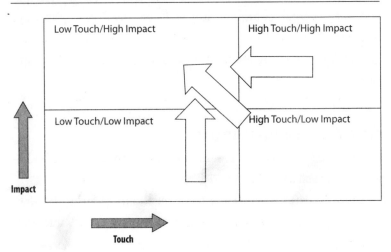

Source: Author.

Internal Communications Brief

One of the easier methods to plan better for internal communications is to use the time-tested brief format. I worked with a
couple of advertising agencies before my internal communications
journey, and the brief helped get everyone on the same page—the
client, the leadership, and internal teams.

THE INTERNAL COMMUNICATIONS BRIEF

The brief collates inputs on specific needs from the communication. Here
is an outline of what can go into a brief that you can use.

1. **Initiative:** What is the background, context, and need?
2. **Expected outcomes:** What does the end result look like?
3. **Audience(s):** Who is the recipient, what do you know about them?
4. **Resources:** What do you need to make this a success: budgets, time, effort?
5. **Messages:** What content is relevant, what will make the audience interested, what do you want them to retain?
6. **Measurement:** How can you gauge success?
7. **Deadline:** By when do you need this started and completed?
8. **Important details:** What needs to positively go in, for example, logo, health plan information, intranet URL, etc?
9. **Pitch:** Does this need to be in the face, subtle, engaging?
10. **Follow-on communication:** What is next? Where does this lead to? How can the campaign be extended?

It is however important to know that brief templates work best
when internal stakeholders are aware of:

1. **How to write them** (It is always helpful to either share
   a completed form as an example or complete the form in
   tandem with the internal client.)
2. **Know what the internal communications team does
   with the form**

3. **The process thereafter to complete the need**
   - The internal communications team also has a part to play when they receive the form.
   - If the form is incomplete or if more information is needed, they need to ask for it.
   - The team needs to identify common themes that emerge from such requests and plan interventions accordingly.
   - They also need to prioritize their tasks based on the level, urgency, and criticality of the tasks and inform stakeholders.
   - Lastly, the team needs to see the 'big picture' and relate each ask to the company's goals.

Internal Communications Channel Selection Chart

The following template allows the internal communicator to select the right channel for the right audience and purpose. The channels will vary depending on your organization but the tool is effective to clearly define what makes sense and at which time (Table 2.2).

Communication Process

Once you have your communication brief in place, you need a process that informs stakeholders on the duration (see Figure 2.5).

So what does good internal communications need to have? Look what this set of best practices call out to get an understanding.

- Open and honest exchanges of information
- Clear, easy-to-understand materials
- Timely distributions
- Trusted sources
- Two-way feedback systems
- Clear demonstrations of senior leadership's interest in employees
- Continual improvements in communication
- Consistent messaging across sources (Solari Communication, 2012).

Table 2.2 Internal Communications Channel Selection Guide

Channel	Format	Audience	Frequency	Owner	Content	Measurement
Company Intranet	Online	All employees or by division	Real-time. Articles posted at the end of every day	Internal Communications	Key company news, project wins, community updates, policies	Page views, usage data, internal communications survey, intranet survey
Newsletter	Web mail and subscriber based	All employees	Released by email	Internal Communications Editor	Strategy, performance, priorities, innovation, and recognition	Internal communications annual survey, readership, articles
Town Halls	Face-to-face	All employees	Quarterly	Leadership Team	Company updates, office news, project progress, recognitions, Q&A	Post session survey
Blogs	Online	All employees	Daily/weekly/fortnightly	Leadership Team	Personal take on hot topics to engage employees	Page views, comments
Videos/ Podcasts	Web	Specific groups	As per need, internal communications team can coach and guide teams to create internal videos	Internal Communications Team	Business and community updates	Views, comments, downloads, listen-ins, comments, direct feedback

Source: Author.

Figure 2.5   Internal Communications Process

Step 1	Step 2	Step 3
Complete and share internal communications brief with team	Discuss brief with IC consultant	IC consultant provides direction, plan, and estimate

Do it yourself model: tools, techniques, local stakeholders' contacts, templates for communication (for example, local initiatives and business communication)

Consultancy: crafting messages, selection of channels, planning, and implementing programme, feedback, metrics (for example, global roll-outs and leadership)

Step 5	Step 4
Roll-out of communication Reporting Plan for follow-up	Sign-off on plan and approval of estimate

Expectation setting on timelines and deliverables |

Source: Author.

PERSPECTIVE

In my involvement in scores of engaging internal communications projects at work, I quickly discovered that planning is the most crucial part of the communication process to derive the maximum results.

As part of the corporate communications team at i-flex, I oversaw the fledgling intranet which went through a redesign, edited the company newsletter, engaged employees with local events and connection programmes, and liaised with the HR for their communication needs.

I was lucky to have worked with the manager at i-flex who had experience with editing and technical writing in his earlier assignments. That helped me learn the ropes of communicating internally. I saw the value of building and improving my writing skills, which I must admit was atrocious during the early part of my stint with internal communications. I also took on additional ownership of corporate social responsibility projects, worked closely with the advertising agency on recruitment marketing and branding effort, and supported leadership visits. This got me more visibility as a leader who can be trusted with the crucial task of enhancing internal communications.

I saw opportunities to build processes that weren't in place, conduct events that connected employees to the organization. When I joined, I was amongst the first members of the team and after 4 years it grew to a larger function that delved into client-facing communication and events.

CASE STUDY

Tele.in is a frontrunner in automobile spare parts and has over 10,000 employees across the globe with a significant multitude based in India.

After 10 years of operations, it now wants to split the company into three business units for better efficiency and managing.

Most of its employees have been with the company for less than 3 years and only a few senior leaders have been with the organization since inception. This new change will also mean a reduction in headcount.

Devise a communication plan to support the Tele.in's leadership team's effort to align employees to their new goal for the firm. Think of the audience's expectations, the scale of operations, the geographic spread, and the modes of communication.

- How will the leadership ensure they do not disengage their employees?
- How can the message be viewed positively?

STUDENT EXERCISE

You are the internal communications contact for Tele.in that plans to launch an employee newsletter. Write a suitable brief using the template provided to explain this new campaign to the design team. Think of creative ways of sharing this message.

CHAPTER 3

Internal Communications Measurement

Measurement plays a crucial role in effective internal communications. To be viewed as a business partner, the internal communications team needs to be proactive in defining how crafting suitable communication interventions leads to direct impact. This chapter articulates the ways to measure the success of internal communications.

In this chapter, I discuss the importance of internal communications measurement, recommendations with metrics, and share tips to get started with online surveys.

A medium-sized IT services firm faced a challenge with information overload. Information overload is not new. According to RescueTime (2008), an organization which analyzes computer use behaviour, a typical information worker who sits at a computer all day turns to his email programme more than 50 times and uses instant messaging 77 times. The research also found that on an average, the worker also opens and reads 40 websites over the course of the day.

Measurement plays a crucial role in effective internal communications. According to the Work Foundation, among the methods used to gauge internal communications' effectiveness are surveys, exit interviews, external audits, and focus group discussions.

I will spend a bit of time explaining how to construct a suitable internal communications survey, one among the most popular measurement techniques.

Internal communications has traditionally been perceived as a support role and a sunk cost. Therefore, very few organizations and leaders have questioned how internal communications generates business results in the long run or even translates into immediate success in the near term.

The closest most measurement metrics aim at is completion rates for communicating messages and the number of times a newsletter has been published.

This is where internal communications misses the bus.

To be viewed as a business partner, the internal communications team needs to be proactive in defining how crafting suitable communication interventions leads to direct impact.

So where does one begin? How do you articulate an internal communications measurement index? How does one get buy-in? What are the ways to measure the success of measurement?

To get started, first list out the objectives you have in mind to measure your internal communications.

The easy ones are to know if you are making progress, to get a good sense of the current state of the business, and keeping a tab on the impact of your work.

I think the key ones are to improve your efficiencies, to be able to get a seat at the table, to be taken seriously by stakeholders, and to improve your team's image as a metrics-driven unit.

The cherry on the cake—measuring changes in behaviour and the value your internal stakeholders get from the internal communications consulting you provide. Let me explain this. As a partner to your stakeholders, you often define tools and resources that empower them to get their work done. How often do we revisit if these are getting used in the way you envisaged? The proof of the pudding is in the eating. If they aren't sticking to standards or making the most of what you provide, it is inevitable that you are going to be on point for their needs every time.

Another scenario—you rolled out a Town Hall and you measured what your staff thought of the content and impact. By taking their feedback a month later, you can gauge if they continue to register the message and are using it in some form.

Here are strategies you can adopt to get the most of your metrics.

Define the different levels of measurement metrics that will make you successful. There can be three levels—your own work and output, the quality and adoption of channels, and stakeholders' ability to be effective.

Revisit your goals as a team. Do you want to improve reach, reduce information overload, enhance understanding, keep things simple, or just define standards? Articulate what you have as success measures to begin your measurement endeavour.

Outline your service-level agreements upfront. Most often stakeholders aren't aware of what they can expect from you and when. Have these listed and published. It builds credibility and transparency to your goals.

Put a number for return on effort. Every single muscle strained to improve your internal communications is an investment towards your goal of getting to the next level.

Begin in your backyard. Before preaching the word on measurement, check if standards and processes are followed effectively in your team. Iron out the concerns before taking measurement out to stakeholders.

Refer statistics and data points from well-researched reports on how improvement in communication helped organizations succeed. Use them to build your own measurement metric. For example, a poorly written headline on your intranet leads to your staff losing time in locating critical information. This directly translates into a loss for your organization if you multiply by the number of people you have.

Get to the low-hanging fruits. Tackle simple mailer open rates to show improvements due to effective communication, frequency, and timing.

Put a weight on standards. While you define your content and design standards, also rate them based in order of importance.

That gives you a yardstick to arrive at a final scorecard to rank your stakeholders on how they are faring.

Report out first, rank later. To get stakeholders into a rhythm, begin by first reporting out how they currently fare. For example, if you have 100 emails hitting your staff every month, identify the key communicators and list their contribution. Over time, release a ranking of where they stand in terms of following standards vis-à-vis impact.

Not everything needs to be measured. If your stakeholders do not have direct control over costs, then sharing a measurement metric which is focused on spending is redundant. It can, however, be used by you as an internal measure.

PERSPECTIVE

Even though the internal communications team had provided guidance on converging communication and leveraging appropriate channels for reaching audiences, many stakeholders felt their messages didn't get visibility. This led them to send out most communication via emails. In the long run, employees began to ignore messages which ranged from 100 to 120 emails a month. To change behaviour and get stakeholders to consider the users' plight, I began reporting out the top three contributors to information overload in my monthly update to stakeholders. It called out the total emails hitting audiences and who were responsible for contributing the maximum emails. This action triggered a change among leaders whose teams were highlighted, and they began questioning their communication champions on how to stem the flow of mailers. At the same time, the report also carried tips on reducing information overload—such as combining mailers, adding updates to the intranet, and leveraging the newsletter. This dual strategy worked only because we were able to use a measurement metric to our advantage.

In summary, what you can probably measure is given in Table 3.1:

Table 3.1 Internal Communications Measurement Elements

Elements	Measures					
IC Department (support function)	Team's satisfaction ratings	Employees' reach	Communication clarity	Hits/views on channels	Adherence to standards	Team's efficiency
Organizational impact	Behaviour change/ Improvement	Channel effectiveness	Leadership credibility	Employee turnover	Awareness levels	Error rate reduction
Stakeholders' output	Team's effectiveness	Compliance	Quality improvement	Timeliness/ consistency	Info overload reduction	Support received ('I feel well supported')
Profit centre (revenue generation)	Number of projects	Client satisfaction rate	Support for other geographies	Revenue generated	Employee turnover	Demand for outsourcing

Source: Author.

Report Out Your Progress

I have often discovered that while most internal communicators do a great job of getting things done, they fail at keeping stakeholders informed on progress, gaps, and issues that need resolution.

One leader told me that since there were many people who join new and have no context on what an internal communications function does or can do, it helps to publish a report on key initiatives, milestones completed, and what's in store for the future.

In short, your report-out can contain the following and be published either weekly/fortnightly/monthly/quarterly.

- progress
- what took place
- impact
- what's coming, metrics

Running an Online Survey

Very often, in our enthusiasm of gauging feedback on the effectiveness of our programmes, we hurriedly put a survey out. Completing such a survey can be time consuming or may not get you relevant inputs, thereby defeating the purpose of creating a survey.

Here are tips and best practices for survey planning, construction, and delivery to the appropriate audience so that you can get the maximum from your responses.

Survey versus Focus Group: If your programme is at an early stage or in its first few cycles, you may want to conduct a focus group rather than a survey, which may be more effective in comparison. A census survey can be attempted for large-scale satisfaction studies.

Survey Audience: People are pressed for time and constantly receive numerous requests for action. Therefore, does your survey need to include the entire community? Or, can you work within a subset?

Connect to Your Programme Objectives: Ensure you have aligned the questions to what you started out to achieve. For example, if the objective of your Town Hall was to engage people, can you convert it into a survey question, 'The Town Hall conducted for Team X helps me feel connected with the community?'

Length of Survey: The survey must be easy to complete and allow respondents to reasonably answer. Grouping similar questions will help respondents to relate better and take the survey sooner. A survey must not take longer than 2–3 minutes to complete unless it is a larger company-wide employee satisfaction feedback where there is a need to drive through improvement action planning at local levels, which requires frontline managers to be provided with their own reports.

Commitment to Action: Articulate your vision for action. Employee buy-in is critical to the success of your survey. If they believe that improvements will result from the survey, they are more likely to participate by completing it and will become actively involved.

PERSPECTIVE

Melcrum's (2009) survey, Key Benchmark Data for Communicators, reveals that only 15 per cent of communication professionals believe they're able to demonstrate the financial return on investment in internal communications. Just over 50 per cent said they're unable to do this and the remaining 35 per cent were unsure.

Among participants of the 2011 India Internal Communications Survey, only 7 per cent responded that they can demonstrate the financial returns of internal communications with stakeholders!

From my experience, the biggest reason why internal communications don't see measurement as important is the lack of accountability on the organization to challenge how the function adds value. Without internal communicators taking the lead in defining what and how to measure, there will also be doubts about the function's effectiveness and impact.

CASE STUDY

Amit, the internal communications personnel assigned to run a Town Hall with the visiting leadership team, is keen to build in measurement metrics to demonstrate the impact of the session. He doesn't have budgets at his disposal but wants to build a case to seek funds for better audiovisual infrastructure, often the reason for such sessions generating less than enthusiastic participation. What measures must Amit arrive at to meet his objectives?

STUDENT EXERCISE

Email is one of the key channels of communication at Agile Biz, a low-cost technology provider with a staff of 4,000 employees across four cities in India. Unfortunately, the internal communications team isn't able to justify how email is meeting the expectations as a channel. Outline your strategy and steps to develop a method that determines the impact of email as a vehicle.

CHAPTER 4

Internal Communicators: Building and Coaching Your Team

The roles and responsibilities of an internal communicator are the effective creation, delivery, measurement, and reporting of employee communication. Building a team is dependent on the competencies expected of the role and need of the organization. In this chapter, we discuss ideas, practices, and recommendations to build, grow, and coach an internal communications team.

In this chapter we discuss ideas, practices, and recommendations to build, grow, and coach your internal communications team. We also explore the debate on outsourcing versus in-sourcing the function.

Internal Communicators—Partnering for Success

The partnership with human resources (HR) is instrumental to the success of the organization since both these groups have a common stakeholder—employees. HR is a stakeholder, but internal communicators do more than just liaison on projects. On the one hand, internal communicators are consultants who guide and coach HR on the nuances of effective communication. HR's core strengths are defining and administering policies and programmes that make the organization a great place to work and supporting any employer branding effort. Internal communicators, on the other hand, also support these initiatives by giving guidance on what works, which channels to use and how to ensure messages reach audiences appropriately and translate into tangible benefits for the organization.

Due to the continued importance of communication, growth of social media, increased span of control and varied scope of the role, the internal communicator is sought after by most internal groups for advice and intervention while engaging potential clients, investors, prospective employees. Their span even includes corporate social responsibility, risk management, information security, office communication, crisis management, communication training, campus communication, and recruitment marketing.

Internal communicators are dedicated to improving continuous two-way flow of communication between the organization and its internal constituents. They support the organization at multiple levels—framing key messages, building and managing communication channels such as intranets and portals, reviewing organizational climate, acting as internal brand custodians, programme managing large company-wide transformational communication programmes, sharing best practices, coaching employees on knowledge sharing, and working as ambassadors of the organization's culture.

Skills, Competencies, and Growth

The roles and responsibilities of an internal communicator are the effective creation, delivery, measurement, and reporting of employee communication. A representative job profile will include supporting the CEO's office, managing editing and publishing content, establishing periodic face-to-face interactions with leadership and employees, overseeing the intranet and usage, monitoring business activities, and instant reporting about newsworthy events to employees, conducting and analyzing internal surveys, collaborating with corporate communication, or marketing with feedback and suggestions related to internal activities.

In this role, knowledge of management theory and practice relevant to sector of operations helps immensely. That includes how communication works, what models exist, how audiences receive information, which channels are effective, and what are the latest trends sweeping the industry and domain.

It is vital to learn more about the local culture and legal issues in communication. Internal communicators are expected to have an eye for detail and ear for local communication and news. They must have the ability to spot opportunities and translate them into concrete, measurable communication.

As an internal communicator, one must also understand the nuances of communication politics and planning, which includes the basics of audience, content, and return of investment.

Among the essential skills expected of an internal communicator are writing, planning, managing complexity, and media management. The softer aspects include influencing, relationship building, networking, listening, process implementation, and professional knowledge. Knowledge of social media, design, photography, and video editing are extremely handy, and today most internal communicators are expected to be experts in these areas.

Building, Growing, and Coaching Your Team

In an HSBC-led study on world class communication, the 1:1,000 ratio of internal communicators to every employee supposedly is a good measure on arriving at the number of team members for an organization (Internal Communications Hub, 2009). However, the ratio expanded to 1:10,000 when the team extended its role across other domains such as external communication.

Building a team is dependent on the competencies expected of the role and need of the organization.

To begin, it is important to know the current challenges which the organization faces, which may be as follows:

- Is engagement waning?
- Is attrition rising?
- Is collaboration an issue?
- Are employees aware of the organization's goals?
- Are employees aligned to where the organization is heading?
- Do they know their role in the organization's success?
- Is trust among leadership dropping?
- Is the basic infrastructure in place?
- Or, are the basics of communication—timely, consistent, relevant, and frequent messages—missing?

There is a myth that in order for coaching to be a success, it should be handled only by leaders, it requires a certification, and also it expects staff to be receptive.

I beg to differ. As communication professionals, we have a responsibility not just to grow ourselves but to also grow the function and the team. This investment pays immense dividends in the long run and the opportunities to coach arrive in all forms and shapes each day. So what are those opportunities? How can you be an effective communication coach?

A competent communication coach needs to be credible: To begin, you need to get a firm grasp of the business and the function. Understanding stakeholders' expectations, studying trends in the industry, gauging winds of change, and gaining trust are among the first few steps one can take to be acknowledged as a coach. By contributing to thought leadership and being viewed as an expert among peers in the industry adds to the overall value you bring as a coach.

Listening intently: Very often we are in such a rush to deliver effectively for stakeholders that we fail to listen to the 'needs'. In a recent episode, a stakeholder keen to improve connection with staff began working on a newsletter. The internal communicator assigned to the business, in all earnest, supported the editing of the draft. However, when I probed on the specific task, it dawned that the stakeholder hadn't the faintest idea about the various channels for promoting messages. His supervisor also pressurized him to get 'something out' to check off their programme list for the quarter. After sharing the pros and cons of launching a newsletter and providing direction on ways to increase awareness, the stakeholder revisited the plan.

51

Spend time providing context: You may have information that helps connect the dots and gives your team line of sight on where the organization is heading. Share what it means to stakeholders to see measurable results from internal communications. Storytelling is a great way to explain the larger picture. However, be aware that the stakeholder may not have enough context or understanding of the subject and it is your responsibility to create awareness of the benefits of effective internal communications. When a stakeholder refused to follow templates created to publish messages, I supported my team member to reinforce the importance of predictability, consistency, and standardization in internal communications and also share the benefits of such an approach. This helped the client appreciate the internal communications perspective and be less resistant to trying the template.

Broaden their horizons: Apart from setting clear objectives and reviewing them periodically (at least every month), it is vital to allow the team to think of problem solving. Get them out of their comfort zones. For example, when the office administration arrived at a concern of non-availability of parking slots as a flare point, the internal communications staffer discussed ways for people to car pool and use feeder services to get to office.

Shifting mindsets—executor to a thought leader: In India where hierarchy plans an important role in how an organization functions, getting the team to think of themselves as thought leaders takes a lot more effort. There is a belief that at the junior level, one needs to only 'execute' what the leader assigns. I encourage the team to embed themselves in key teams, get to know power users of communication, and coach them to co-create content. The expectation is that in the long run, we wean off stakeholders from viewing us as a production unit that churns out communication. It also helps them feel more in control of their assets, builds internal communications capabilities, and enhances their experience.

Lead by example: To be able to coach your team to success, the leader needs to set exemplary examples. Be it in influencing decisions, taking the team along through change, working through difficult scenarios, and bringing key people together. If you expect the team to have an open mind, you must first be willing to listen to different perspectives, even if they may sound unviable. Recently, I had the opportunity to draw a framework for a leadership forum and guide how leaders focused their energies. Although the challenges of managing varied perspectives (and egos!) got frustrating at times, I picked up key behaviours of leaders that later provided my team insights to leverage.

Acknowledge your drawbacks: A coach isn't expected to be perfect. By acknowledging your gaps, you are also demonstrating commitment to learn. While editing drafts, I often get confused while using the words 'advice' versus 'advise' in my sentences. After reading up the difference, I shared my personal learning with the team.

Make things simple: After drawing their attention to the big picture, you need to help them break it down to smaller action steps. This includes giving guidance on setting suitable objectives, talking with other team members, connecting with the local support teams, interacting with people from the industry, meeting with leaders, and last but not least looking inwards at their own strengths and capabilities. Point to them literature on the web, your intranet, best practices, key websites that share insights, etc.

Engaging for growth: Coaching the team involves helping them to be better individuals as well as better team players. Therefore, help identify opportunities where they can lead the way (maybe conducting trainings, workshops) or become better at building assets for stakeholders. Involve them in crafting a working list of initiatives they can own and deliver—with minimal supervision. Provide inputs on process, effort, measurement, among other specifics.

Coaching takes time and it isn't a one-off exercise. If you are committed to growing the team (and it will show), there is no better way than to begin right away.

Internal Communications Maturity Guide

If you already have a team and are keen to know where you stand in terms of maturity, look up Table 4.1. The chart helps you

Table 4.1 Internal Communications Maturity Guide

Basic	Intermediate	Advanced
You have a basic communication plan	You have a structured communication plan with a strategy and implementable ideas	Your team consists of experts and specialists
Your leadership is invested in the team		You have a sophisticated measurement index
You have simple ways to measure your impact	You have robust measurement indices	You are enlisted as a coach to guide leaders and teams
There is limited or no knowledge sharing within the team	You have clear business goals	Your team is embedded or tightly aligned with business
Team members are generalists	You are able to position your department with leaders to engage and influence decision-making	You are able to derive an ROI for your communication
	Your projects are fairly complex	You are core to informing business leaders on culture and emerging trends

Source: Author.

understand your internal communications function standing in the organization set-up. Which bucket does your team fall in?

Building your Internal Communications Team's Presence

Internal communicators are experts and specialists who collaborate with leaders and human resources to help achieve a common understanding, build connection, and recognize employees. There are numerous benefits of consistent internal communications such as enhanced productivity, greater commitment, improved working environment, lower turnover, increased customer orientation, and better business growth. However, to be accepted as leaders, the team needs to prove its worth. Here are some ways to ensure you can coach your team and build presence.

Have your team's interest on your radar: To be effective with internal communications means to be able to set the right expectations on the role and impact. Very often the team is small as compared to other support groups and therefore it is helpful to set service level agreements (SLAs) for all the work you offer. You will do your team a favour by explaining your team's role at every opportunity you get. Have an outreach presentation which articulates what the internal communications team stands for, supports in terms of work and stakeholders, and showcase recent cases where you have bought about tangible impact.

Deliver on time: Nothing beats the ability to delight your stakeholders. I have often found that when you consistently deliver quality solutions on time, your credibility goes up.

Be seen as a thought leader: If you are a team leader, you are in the best position to identify opportunities for learning and development both internally and externally. Coach them on conducting events and workshops. The more your team is seen as leading the way with thoughtful recommendations, there are greater chances of it getting the right support. For example, there will be opportunities to share best practices in internal communications, discuss ways to plan communication better, create digital storytelling assets, improve writing standards, use social media effectively, and craft suitable messages. These are obviously skills that many stakeholders will love to have.

Value-add over and beyond role: I often encourage my team to go over and above their work and participate in not just internal forums but also external sessions. There is no better way to expand perspective and broaden horizons. Have them join local communication groups, team up with corporate social responsibility units, or even contribute articles to publications.

Team structure: Revisit your team structure to check if there is enough cross-pollination and collaboration. Often teams work in silos only because their line of sight is limited. Get everyone on the same page either with periodic updates or calls. Have team members work on cross-departmental themes where better ideas are germinated.

Periodic updates: Apart from the outreach presentation, it helps to periodically send out a report. I practise a highly successful monthly report-out to stakeholders which covers the highlights of the previous month, the stakeholders impacted, metrics from the communication interventions, feedback, and a snapshot on what's coming next. I also ensure to call out success stories, challenges, key people who contributed, and the outcomes we are driving towards. It is useful to ask for feedback on the report so that you can continue improvising. One important feedback that I recently incorporated related to what the internal communications team does. The feedback came in that very few were aware of the offerings that internal communications had as a service.

Reporting out event results: Some report-outs may not be able to wait till the monthly cycle, so you may need to publish sooner. It can be a recent event.

External trends and outcomes: Share positive and negative sentiments on topics of relevance. For example, an attrition study that depicts how the region or a certain industry is faring. You can review and synthesize a Great Place to Work Survey report and provide directions.

Page on your intranet: Have a page on your internal network where stakeholders and employees get to know your team, the work you do, the policies, the process, the format, and how to join hands with your team. You may have a project which needs audience participation. This is a great way to start.

Build case studies on great work: You can explain most of what you do through relevant and insightful case studies. Be it how you promoted a leadership visit, a change management intervention where you overcome mindsets, or a crisis communication which reduced impact to the organization.

Recognize people who supported your team: It is probably the easiest but often very likely missed in an increasingly fast-paced world—recognizing those who make your team excel. As a support function, you will be working closely with the office departments to extend the reach and impact of your communication. The people behind the scenes are the one who need a pat on their back.

Communicating a common voice: Finally, does your team have a shared understanding of what you stand for and deliver? I am often surprised that internal communications leaders overlook this very important element of building team presence. Have an elevator speech that everyone on the team knows and can articulate well. It is also important that each member knows what the other is doing, either through knowledge sharing sessions or by reaching out during 1:1s.

Outsourcing versus In-sourcing

Very often I come across questions on communication social networks asking for recommendations on good internal communications agencies to work with.

After having worked with agencies and independently as an in-sourced team, I am convinced that the latter model works best.

Let us however explore the pros and cons of both models for you to take an informed decision.

Before we get there, let us identify the elements and reasons why organizations outsource their internal communications needs.

Most often, elements that are outsourced are communication design, content writing, event management, and communication implementation. These range from keeping costs low to focusing on core areas of work.

Most often elements that are outsourced are communication design, content writing, event management, and communication implementation. Reasons range from keeping costs low to focusing

Table 4.2 Outsourcing versus In-sourcing Matrix

Strategy	Pros	Cons
Outsourcing	Reduced overhead costs, less manpower on company, ability to focus on core areas, can change agencies based on performance, outside in perspectives	Reduced accountability, inability to understand organization's culture and needs, recurring costs, confidentiality concerns, works best if there is an account manager from the agency who liaises with the internal communications manager
In-sourcing	Better control, ability to share sensitive information with team, reduced costs for design, printing, etc., output and copyright are proprietary, opportunity to manage quality and process, faster time to market	Tougher to grow team, need for investments in learning and development, lack perspectives from the external world

Source: Author.

on core areas of work. Though, having an in-source team aligns better with the organization's goals, as it can work on sensitive information and deliver swiftly (see Table 4.2).

SELECTING THE RIGHT AGENCY

If you are taking the outsourcing route, it helps to be on the same page with your stakeholders while selecting your agency. Therefore, having the right benchmarks will allow you to set expectations and make the right choice. Here are some sample templates which will enable you to compare and contrast agencies (see Tables 4.3 and 4.4).

Table 4.3 Agency Selection Template—Before Pitch

Agency Name	Credentials	Address	Website URL	email ID	Contact Person	Escalation Contact	Offices across Locations	Recent Campaigns	References
	Year established, private/public organization, number of years in business, number of clients, turnover								

Source: Author.

Table 4.4 Agency Selection Template—After Pitch

Internal Communications Agency Pitch Evaluation		Agency A	Agency B	Agency C	Agency D
This format helps internal communicators evaluate the strength of the agency based on agreed parameters	Weightage				
Capabilities/cross location expertise	10				
Understanding of company's requirement	20				
Presentation	10				
Robustness of idea/differentiators	10				
Reference check	10				
Final Score					
Decision to go with (yes/no/keep on file)					

Source: Author.

It is important to establish the rationale for selection of the agency for improved transparency.

Your Role as Client While Briefing an Agency

The reason why client companies employ and pay ad agencies is because they enable solving of brand problems and exploit brand opportunities.

Clients employ advertising agencies because they help solve branding issues and exploit opportunities. Since advertising is a function designed to achieve specific goals, it becomes essential to provide a good brief to expect a good outcome.

Why is the brief so important? Due to the fact that much time and effort are going to be spent on the campaign, it provides the organization and agency an opportunity to create something that works and the ownership to ensure that it does.

But it's important for the client to know the advertising development process—a kind of relay race.

One, the departments which are involved and how they go about it. This becomes essential so as to be able to gauge the time taken for creative work to develop.

Two, for the client to know where exactly he can play a pivotal role in the strategy development.

Strategic development involves understanding the clients' business, their consumers, their marketplace, and their brand. It forms an important part of the creation briefing as it represents the stage in the advertising development process where the strategic understanding developed by the account team reaches the people whose job it is to crack the creative problem.

But this strategic understanding has to be translated into a form which is a useful tool and inspiration for the creative team.

All advertising does not work. Even though we would make this assumption that all advertising works.

The truth is that some work and some don't. Creative briefing is one of the surest ways to ensure that the possibilities of it working are high. You can view creative briefing as a lever that can be tugged at a particular direction giving it a different result each time. You can also view it as the rudder to a ship or oil to an engine.

Then comes the tone of voice. This needs to be defined. Should it be heroic, aristocratic, formal, casual, or charged? This is important, as it would affect the final output of the communication.

Briefs Should Be Simple and to the Point

You should be able to explain it in layman's terms.

There is a brief and a briefing: Brief forms the written communication which goes to the creative team; briefing is the dialogue, discussion, and direction which occur around the brief. The client plays part in both, adding definition.

Brief should be having two key properties—directional and inspirational. Directional is where the client can play a prominent role. Not to discount the role in inspiring the agency.

Directional—means it should define the task—what the advertising needs to achieve, the problem it is trying to solve.

Inspirational—means giving the creative team a springboard, a jumping off point. Here 'feel', 'tone of voice', 'look', and 'effect' should be taken into account.

63

Sections of the brief can be defined as per the following areas:

Why are we communicating? What is the role of advertising? What is the advertising doing? What do we want people to think?

Who are we talking to? Target group. Type and outlook of person, not just demographics. Their behaviour with respect to our objectives.

What are we saying? Perspective/main thought + support.

How are we saying it? Tone of voice—adult to adult, parent to a parent.

- Brand identity
- Executive guidelines—Things to avoid. Things to do
- Request—Media consideration/requirement
- Timings

Refer to Chapter 2 for the internal communications brief template.

To sum up, the client can play an important role in enhancing the creative briefing by participating actively in the process, direction, and management.

CASE STUDY

Your company wants to communicate the importance of a dress code to your employees since they are noticing most your staff are coming in sandals and ill-fitting dresses. This is a cause of embarrassment, especially when clients visit the organization and it has a detrimental effect on the image of the company.

What will be your advice to the HR partner who wants to highlight this important message?

How will you ensure it is followed?

STUDENT EXERCISE

Conduct a comprehensive study of how companies conduct new joiner orientation and make the 'first day at work' a fantastic experience.

CHAPTER 5

Internal Communications in India

Internal communications for a long time has been considered and treated as a very trivial function in India, and there is also a paucity of research on this topic. However, with the entry of multinationals, there has been a greater understanding of the role internal communications plays in driving connection and engagement among employees. This chapter also discusses the ways in which Indian organizations are able to align employees through the effective use of internal communications.

In this chapter, I discuss various perspectives of internal communications practised in India. I also share insights from leaders based on a web-based study conducted.

There is a paucity of research on internal communications in India. At best there are anecdotal references in newspapers and publications that relate to specific topics such as employee engagement, social media, and role of HR in communication. There are also a few case studies on the subject that refer to internal communications from a change management context. The value of internal communications and the range of expectation are rarely discussed.

I conducted a web-based study among seven India-based internal and corporate communication leaders to gauge their understanding of the range and expectations, challenges and issues, new media and implications, internal communications and crises, and working with agencies. Below is a summary of their perspectives. These leaders were picked on the basis of their knowledge, proven expertise, and experience in the industry. Out of the 15 leaders I approached, seven sent in their completed forms.

Range and Expectations of Internal Communications

Leaders believe that internal communications is meant to inform, connect, recognize, motivate, and engage employees. Among the expectations of internal communications is to improve collaboration, increase alignment, foster an environment of change, and innovate and give employees a platform to give back to the community.

Among the essentials of internal communications are consistency, transparency, 'human touch', and tone of voice.

The role of the internal communicator is seen as someone who can advise leaders on the communication process, align employees to company goals, improve internal brand recall, support change management, and help keep the culture of the organization consistent. Among the most popular media are intranet, email, Town Halls, and newsletters.

This, however, seems inconsistent with what practitioners believe are roles expected to be played by an internal communicator. Sample these direct comments from a recent study, 2011 India Internal Communications Survey (Verghese, 2011).

'Create a sense of ownership and engagement within the organization.'

'Enthuse, engage and empower amongst others!'

'Keep employees informed, engaged and entertained.'

'Help leadership and HR drive employee engagement.'

It is obvious that a gap exists on what the function can do and a lot more effort is needed to bridge the understanding.

How Has the Role Changed?
Internal communications has changed from being a 'command and control' to a 'collaborative' model. Internal communications has been often seen as a less than important function, although today the role is more inclusive and that is reflected in how issues are discussed and seek feedback.

The internal communications experts consider the role and expectations of the function dramatically shifting.

Here are a few comments from leaders:

'Internal communication for a long time has been considered and treated as a very trivial function. Today, fortunately that trend and perception has changed. The board is keen to understand employees better and engage with them to realize their ambitions and potential.'

'Today, internal communications is a specialized function, where the CXO spends time with professionals to understand how he can connect with his employees to drive home and into their hearts the message he wants to deliver.'

Leaders listen to employees and discuss relevant themes that internal communicators address, such as cultural sensitivities, organizational climate, messages, speed, and creativity of communication. Organizations are also willing to understand the potential of employees. There is increased pressure to share more and more information about how organizations are faring, therefore, companies seek expert advice. Winning the hearts and minds of employees is now crucial, and internal communications is thus viewed as an important function. Building a strong culture is critical today for organizations. Organizations are keen to manage informal channels such as the grapevine and internal communicators are expected to be adept with sophisticated technology such as video conferencing, vodcasts, blogs, etc. Blogs are perceived to support open communication.

Most agree that face-to-face works best as the channel to share messages while managers are expected to play a leading role.

Governance, ethics, and transparency are themes that emerged as important in today's context.

Challenges Facing Internal Communications

Due to how the function is perceived, the team is often tasked with a set of 'to-dos'. This makes the function seem very tactical. Although technological advances and newer tools have made communication easier and reduced geographical barriers, it has also impacted 'human touch'.

In an increasing complex world, the inability to keep things simple has also a profound impact on how communication is understood. Cultural contexts and sensitivities lead to misinterpretations of messages. Examples of these include the mode of communication such as email, accent, and dressing.

The attitude of communicators, inability to add value, viewing communication holistically from the employees' viewpoint, and lack of understanding from senior leadership are often barriers to the impact of internal communications.

Leaders identified messaging, building culture, and establishing consistency as areas that need more focus. The inability to engage or involve the 'frozen middle'—a reference for the manager community—is seen as a drawback.

Managing New Media Challenges

Newer modes of communication and the influence of social media have challenged internal communicators to think differently.

Newer modes of communication and the influence of social media have challenged internal communicators to think differently. It is encouraging yet sometimes worrying for communicators to know that employees can choose their information, form opinions, and participate in conversations independently and without consulting anyone. The role of the internal communicator is to help employees make sound judgement, communicate effectively in two-way conversations, and stay connected and well informed.

The speed, transparency, and non-regulation of content is discomforting for communicators.

Language barriers, lack of planning, untested crisis communication, and inability to track usage across all sites make it difficult for communicators to grasp the complete implications of new media.

There is also cynicism about the channels and their usage.

For example, a leader commented that 'corporate blogs are overrated'—most company blogs are self-serving and comments are 'politically correct reactions that really don't take the debate forward in any significant way'.

It seems that podcasts are better received in India, since companies are comfortable with one-way communication.

Multinational Companies in India and Internal Communications

With the entry of multinationals to India, there has been a greater understanding of the role internal communications plays in driving connection and engagement among employees. With their experience and proven practices, it is easier for them to get into a region and adopt sooner. The multinational companies (MNCs) in India are best positioned to make the most of internal communications by leveraging their scale, scope, and intellectual capital.

Their entry also did change the talent landscape with candidates able to identify to aspirational values showcased by these organizations. The multinationals offer better career opportunities and salaries for candidates and although finally people work for people, the organizational identity does have an influence on the choice.

Leaders felt that Indian companies wanting to expand abroad should pick best practices from multinationals. One of the challenges organizations in India grapple with is attrition, and the role of internal communications is to support existing employees in being aware of the promise and potential of the company and articulate why they need to stay with the organization. The need for reinforcing the employee value proposition is much greater now.

Getting Buy-in from Senior Management—Issues and Recommendations

Leaders felt that demonstrating value is most important to get a seat at the table.

Have a measurement matrix to showcase progress and impact. Leaders felt that demonstrating value is most important to get a seat at the table. They have a measurement matrix to showcase progress and impact, which also demonstrates communication return on investment and improvement in employees' interest levels.

Before you approach leadership, you should have a concrete plan. Build your reason and know the results you want to achieve.

Internal communications proposals must highlight how you are making employees a part of the process while building a business case for benefits.

Having a 1:1 relationship with the management is very crucial for the success of any internal communications initiative.

The leadership must be a believer, demonstrate genuine interest in people, work closely with HR, think creatively, listen, and observe organizational action at close quarters.

The internal communications plan must include goals, resources, decision-makers, and budgets.

Engaging an External Agency for Internal Communications—Attributes and Roles

According to leaders, having an external agency to support your internal communications works best when both parties work with agreed calendar, goals, resources, budgets, and measurable deliverables. The agency needs to be seen as an extension of creativity and production for the internal communications team.

Among the attributes that organization should look for are cross-industry insights, proven experience, proof of transformational communication, ability to write for global audiences, and the expertise to develop content. It is expected that the agency brings best practices and innovations to the table. Mostly design and copy expertise are outsourced. Newsletters and videos are often artefacts that are produced by agencies.

The model works well when the internal communications knows the business context and the external agency delivers to the brief. The internal communications contact is expected to understand the pulse of the organization and relate to people. The agency always will make it a priority if there are better revenue streams.

Best Practices and Case Studies from India

There are some interesting case studies emerging from India in the recent past.

Frauenheim (2005) outlines the case of HCL Technologies that shifted the way employees perceived their commitment to the organization. With a new company philosophy, 'Employee First, Customers Second', the focus was on a better experience for the employees, which resulted in more accountability, better communication with the CEO. The new approach led to curtailed attrition and generated fast revenue growth. The company also encouraged employees to communicate directly with the CEO. Through the programme *U&I*, the CEO answered 100 questions from workers each week, creating an open and healthy work atmosphere, conducive for improved communication climate.

Sudhakar and Patil (2006) discussed a case study at Tata Chemicals Ltd, where internal communicators created a Communication Effectiveness Index (CEI) meant to give direction and help the team focus and meet objectives. The team measured the effectiveness rather than the efficiency of the process. Using a questionnaire to gauge the impact of communication, an index for each service business unit (SBU), location, and level of responsibility was arrived at. The findings indicate that employees who were better informed were more committed to seeing the organization succeed. Employees also needed to know that the organization cared for them, that their opinions mattered, and that the company took action.

Bajaj (2008) wrote about a case of Tasty Bites Eatable Ltd (TBEL), where internal communications transformed a good manufacturing company to a high-quality food marketing firm through the active involvement and conversion of its staff to align to the company's objectives. Internal communications interventions included CEO–staff interactions, values and company strategy announcements, and social change messages.

Business Standard Reporter (2009) addressed an internal communications initiative by India's leading Bank—the State Bank of India—to align its people to their goals. The communication aimed at attitudinal change and transformation of its employees through a series of human resources activities. Knowledge sharing was one of the key drivers of the change. The project was conducted in four stages: citizen orientation, customer fulfilment, market engagement, and a vision programme. It aimed at gaining senior management citizenship and hoped to transform the organization. The bank which had launched project 'Parivartan' in 2007—a 100-day programme to increase communication skills of its managers—sees the new project as an extension of the previous one.

HCL Comnet (2005) claimed their internal radio, Radio Comnet, as the world's first 'radio newsletter' in use for the company's internal communications. The radio capsule packages internal corporate news with an entertainment quotient for impactful message delivery. They got a popular radio jockey (RJ) from Mumbai, India, to launch the radio. Unlike an ordinary radio channel, this medium plays pre-recorded messages related to company's latest happenings, news, and also provides an interactive platform to employees to communicate within the company. All this along with popular songs and played as CDs, without using airwaves. Considering that the average age of an employee at Comnet was 25–26 years in 2005, it did seem like a good move to 'involve' staff.

In 2007, Infosys' intranet was named among 'World's 10 Best Intranets' by Nielsen Norman Group, a user experience research firm that advises companies on human-centred product and service design. Infosys became the first Indian company to be selected for the Group's Intranet Design Annual Award (Infosys, 2007).

These cases showcase how Indian organizations are able to align employees through the effective use of internal communications.

CASE STUDY

Janet, an internal communicator with a pharmaceutical firm, feels overwhelmed by the rising demands for her services. It isn't just her organization's managing director who wants her to craft emails, even her supervisor expects her to churn out content for the intranet daily. She begins to feel like a 'postman' who is merely delivering communication. How can you as a leader in her team support her stakeholders to get more value from her role?

STUDENT EXERCISE

You joined recently as an internal communications manager and you are expected to put together best practices from the Indian industry. How will you go about the assignment? What questions will you ask respondents? How will you present your recommendations to your leadership team?

CHAPTER 6

Challenges and Opportunities in Internal Communications

The internal communications practice is quite nascent and, therefore, there is immense potential for growth and learning. Unfortunately, limited investment in developing strategic thinking and planning, creating standards, improving professional's learning, and lack of measurement are stifling growth. This chapter details the various challenges and opportunities that exist in the field of internal communications.

Internal communications is a fast growing function. While there is immense potential and opportunities, often those who plan to make a career in this function aren't aware of the expectations and responsibilities that come with the role. This chapter discusses these issues and more.

Credibility and respect for the practice are necessary for it to blossom. The internal communications practice is quite nascent and therefore there is immense potential for growth and learning. Some organizations prefer a 'one person—fits all' approach—expecting a professional handling public relations (PR) to also manage internal communications. Sometimes, HR owns it and sometimes the executive office. It is quite rare to have a separate entity driving internal communications, which is possibly the best way forward.

Often the expectation is to manage more with the limited set of professionals and those who do not have the relevant experience or interest are saddled with the responsibility of internal communications. There is also a perception that internal communications doesn't make an 'impact' unlike a PR or an event management activity; therefore, this practice gets limited attention, often at the organization's peril. Very few professionals are keen to focus on this specific domain due to a lack of visibility it provides for the individual. Also, organizations believe it is a skill that anyone can have without investing in skills and experience.

Today there is more emphasis to build expertise for this practice, but unfortunately it is rarely taught as a separate subject in management institutions in the country. At best, it is combined under a larger Marketing and Communications module.

Employee engagement is a hot topic in retaining the best talent across industries globally, and internal communicators are 'thought leaders' who advise HR and leaders on strategies. They articulate the need for executive presence, cascading internal messages, and championing internal campaigns and events.

Unfortunately, limited investment in developing strategic thinking and planning, creating standards, improving professional's learning, and lack of measurement are stifling growth.

The other challenge internal communicators face is information overload. Today, a professional is overwhelmed with so much information that they are unable to make sense of it completely. The internal communicator is expected to coach employees and provide leaders with alternate solutions to ensure messages are received, understood, and acted upon.

Apart from these concerns, managing grapevine as a channel of communication, measuring return on investment for communication, and building suitable social tools internally are top of mind for internal communicators.

Growing as an Internal Communicator

The entry-level expectations for the internal communicator are to have direct experience in organizing communication programmes and delivering tangible results. The individual must have supported colleagues in appreciating the quality of communication, encouraged participation on internal communications channels and tools, written messages for a variety of media, and influenced decision-makers on the objectives and measurement of communication. Most internal communications requirements are advertised as word of mouth referrals, and therefore professionals entering this domain may come in with experience in journalism, event management, content writing, PR, and marketing.

At the next stage, also known as the specialist level, the individual is expected to own and manage medium-sized programmes within business groups, demonstrate expertise in translating briefs into concrete interventions, drive adoption of messages, and periodically review channels for consistency.

Moving up the ladder will require the individual to be adept at relationship building with senior stakeholders, supporting change management efforts, conducting focus groups and surveys that help stakeholders gauge pulse of their employees, tackle tough human resources issues, collaborate across teams to maximize the impact of communication.

As the role matures, the internal communicator will need to establish frameworks, think ahead of the curve by identifying trends shaping the future of the workplace, assign value to communication goals, build accountability to communication impact, and think like a business leader.

The career path is well defined and an experienced professional can grow to lead internal communications teams with designations ranging from a director to a senior vice president. Internal communications today is a powerful domain and has a seat at the table on most company boards and leadership teams.

Internal communicators are also aligned by business based on their level of expertise and interest areas. Therefore, you may see opportunities to service internal business needs in groups such as technology, consulting, business process outsourcing, and marketing management.

Apart from the core functions, there are other specific positions available for those interested in joining the internal communications team. These include designers, client liaisons, recognition managers, community relation managers, content writers, corporate citizenship officers, internal branding specialists, leadership coach, leadership communicator, social media integrator, culture communicators, HR communication managers, internal researchers, intranet managers, international business communicators, newsletter editors, and internal event managers.

Joining the Internal Communications Team

The professional seeking an opportunity in this domain is expected to have an excellent knowledge of English, great listening skills, have a background in one of the marketing communication functions, good drafting and copy-editing skills, expertise with online and social media tools, deep knowledge of the industry, and understanding of cultural and legal nuances in communication. At the entry level in India, the internal communicator can expect to earn close to ₹2–3 lakhs per annum.

For students and practitioners interested in entering this field, there is always a debate in their minds on being a specialist versus a generalist. Getting deeper into a domain has its pros and cons. On the one hand, specializing in and focusing on one field or in area can limit your learning and exposure in others. On the other hand, internal communications as a domain will always be around as a need and career if there are organizations who believe in improving employee engagement and increasing business value.

How professionals begin their career in this function continues to be a topic of discussion. In India and these parts people who enter this field usually come in with a knowledge of PR, advertising, corporate communications, journalism, direct marketing, or event management. Or even a combination of all these! Very often internal communications is just another element in their portfolio within the corporate communication function they handle. Leadership traits are an asset, especially since most leaders look to the internal communicator to own and drive a lot more than is expected of their immediate span of control. By demonstrating the ability and confidence to manage corporate assets such as intranets, newsletters, employee engagement programmes, and leadership messaging, one can gradually be entrusted with larger responsibilities in internal communications.

Know What Organizations Seek from Internal Communicators

When it comes to hiring someone for an internal communications job, the following ideas and recommendations can help you choose the right candidate. I have used it while evaluating candidates.

According to me, it boils down to what I call the '3Ds'— individual Driven, Direct, and Distinguished.

Driven—Is the candidate showing enough evidence of initiative and commitment?

Direct—Is the candidate talking to the point? If you can't explain your point crisply, how can you communicate widely with your internal and external stakeholders?

Distinguished—Has the candidate proved his or her worth in the domain?

If you have begun your career, you may argue that you don't have enough reasons and opportunities to make a mark. I disagree. If you are keen to make a mark and be recognized in your field of work, you should have begun early. Nothing stops you from building your portfolio of work even as a freelancer, enrolling for courses, joining a communication body, gaining experience with, say, a non-governmental organization (NGO)—without pay, penning articles for your local newspaper, writing a blog, hosting a photo feature, showcasing your video skills, demonstrating your leadership skills at your college event, or building your personal brand online.

Now coming to the questions I prefer asking during an interview. I try to holistically gauge the candidate at the following levels:

- personal (education, interest, hobbies, etc.)
- team (how they fit into the current scheme of things, how they engage with their team, whom they look to for insights and learning, whom do they report to, how do they manage work)
- organization (how are they making an impact to your organization, how do they know if they are doing so)
- career (expectations, understanding, and awareness of opportunities available)
- industry (how aware are they of trends and impact)
- learning (what investment have they taken to grow, what are they doing to continuously learn more, do they have any mentors)
- personal attributes (how confident are they, is there clarity of thought, what are their impressions on ethics)
- community (what are they doing to improve things around themselves, in everyday life, what steps have they taken to make a difference)

At this point, let me share some pointers on what one should avoid when applying and interviewing for a position.

1. **Stating an incorrect designation and role:** I noticed one curriculum vitae (CV) that changed the current designation and role to suit the profile applied for. I only discovered this when I probed further that the candidate didn't have the relevant experience.

2. **Never bad mouth your current firm:** When I asked what would make the individual switch companies, the answer that I got shocked me! The candidate used phrases like 'lax attitude', 'not going anywhere here', and 'does not matter how long I stay, nothing will change'. Which organization would want to hire someone who has such an attitude? Even if you are getting a raw deal in your current workplace, be thankful for the opportunities you get every day to influence people and the work you do every day.

3. **Unclear about what the industry wants:** If you are keen on making a mark in your area of work, you should positively know what is going on in your industry and the impact of regulations and governmental interventions. I made it a point to ask every candidate about recent trends they observed, and I never got any convincing answers. If you don't know of recent shifts in the way communication is evolving, how do you plan to value-add to how communication is done in your role?

4. **Lack of clarity on career progression:** It is the candidate's responsibility to find out career paths and opportunities that exist in different organizations from literature that is available. There are tons of materials that one can refer to.

5. **Beating around the bush:** If you don't know an answer, say so. No one is expected to know everything, but the least I would expect is that the candidate tells me that he or she would find out, get my contact ID, and let me know. When the expectation is to give simple, direct answers, nothing can be more frustrating than listening to a candidate who beats around the bush.

6. **Wanting to do other jobs within the company:** While candour is appreciated, if you know the role does not suit you, explain it and drop off. I came across a candidate who wanted to play to her strengths in PR when the job clearly

didn't expect her to do so. You first need to prove your worth with what you are asked to do and then move to other domains if you get the opportunity.

7. **Lack of interest in learning more:** I was taken aback when candidates told me that they had absolutely no idea where to seek information on corporate communication or internal communications! It may have been excused 10–15 years ago when the understanding of communication was nascent. Today with a wide spectrum of options to source information from, it is foolish to mention that one has no context! Even a simple Google search will get you all the content you need for a lifetime.

8. **Do not place content in your CV that you can't explain:** If you mention 'objectives' or 'strengths' in your CV, be prepared for questions related to them. For example, one candidate included 'networking skills' and I probed further for an example. Unfortunately, the candidate wasn't able to give me a good example of a networking skill she leveraged to improve her standing. My recommendation is to drop these elements which bloat your CV length. Strengths will be discovered during the course of a conversation.

9. **Don't miss out on your manners:** If you are in a place with a lot of background noise, excuse yourself and buy more time or do the call later. Also ensure you thank the interviewer for his or her time before signing off. Find out if you can continue keeping the relationship going in the future or if you can be mentored by the interviewer if you are convinced about the credentials.

Interview Tips While Applying for an Internal Communications Role

Seeking a role in internal communications and not sure how to go about the interview process?

Here I share pertinent themes and relevant questions that you should ask and seek answers for while planning your move and interviewing for a role in internal communications.

When it comes to a job in internal communications, I will primarily request for a job description of the role from either the consultant or from the company, if you are approached directly. Look for specific asks on collaboration, reporting, success factors, skills, capabilities, opportunities, and growth.

Before you meet the interviewer, you need to be aware of what the organization does and how you fit in. Make it a point to look up the company website—the About Us, Careers, Leadership, Services, Recognitions, and Culture sections provide useful insights about how the organization fares.

Go prepared: Carry samples of your work to share if you believe it will help give a better perspective. I personally find it relevant to explain the outputs and outcomes of communication created. Make sure to give suitable credits to team members and leaders who have coached and guided you in creating the artefacts. Avoid leaving samples behind—considering most internal communications material are proprietary matter of your employer and it will only create doubts in the minds of interviewer about your ethics.

Be upfront: Unless you have decided to make a change, be sure to explain in no uncertain terms that you are exploring the opportunity and the decision to make the move will depend on a variety of factors ranging from role to benefits. Broad themes to focus on while seeking information about the job include the maturity of the role, current state of affairs, your immediate supervisor, learning opportunities, stakeholders, expectations, measure of success, company culture, flexibility, and benefits. You may not be able to ask your questions—so if time runs out or if you think of some more queries, after the interviews please inform the interviewer that you will seek further inputs by email or through the consultant, whichever approach is suitable to the interviewer.

Role maturity: Try to understand where internal communications sits in the organization. Is it with the CEO's office, HR, within a function, a part of marketing, or as a separate entity? It may be that this is a new role (especially if it is an MNC and they are expanding local operations). Decide what is the need and why does it require filling now. Does internal communications have a seat at the table?

Current state of affairs: You must probe what makes the role important, the perception of internal communications among people, what will help overcome the gaps, what are the top three priorities of the leadership in the near and long terms.

Your immediate supervisor: Research reports have proven that employees leave managers, not organizations. Make it a point to personally meet and engage with the person you will directly work with and who will review your performance. Make an attempt to understand your manager's background, credibility, and key strengths. Have you Googled your supervisor's name and checked?

Opportunities for learning: Get a grasp of what's in it for you when it comes to personal learning. Is the role going to sharpen your core skills, provide you ample opportunities to expand networks, access knowledge and to become a better professional?

Know your stakeholders: Make it a point to learn more about whom you will interact with every day and who will be responsible for your success in the firm.

Expectations at work: Seek and understand what 'a day in the life of the communicator' is like in the organization. How much time goes in your core work and other ancillary activities?

Success measures: Very often how you define success is what you will be supporting in your communication. Therefore, it is vital to understand the ways stakeholders measure successes. More importantly, how does your manager understand it?

Growth opportunities: How does it all add up and link to your career aspirations? Figure how much of investment the organization does for growing people within the system.

Company's background: Think about why you are seeking the opportunity with this organization—is it the work, the brand, the culture, compensation, role, designation, flexibility? Maybe a combination of factors. However, just be sure you got it right before saying yes. Talk to people in the industry, ask around in the same organization, and discuss your concerns with the consultant.

Culture and context: Very often the culture of the organization can help you fit in or stand out like a sore thumb. Ensure you have got enough context on what makes the place tick. Get a pulse of how it is to work in there. Look out for warning signs when you walk in for discussions—the way employees greet each other, their leaders, how leaders engage with peers and subordinates. Also, how comfortable people look while going about their work. Find out how things work, what made them join, how they perceive the firm vis-à-vis their former employer. Trawl social networking sites and www.glassdoor.com for comments and feedback on the company's background and policies.

Before you take the leap: Think about opportunities lost at your current workplace and if the new employer is willing to compensate for the change or for the losses. Be open and flexible however when the decision is taken, since it may not always be a win-win situation.

Prepare for questions: Be ready for queries such as:

- Why do you want this job?
- Why are you moving?
- Samples of work you have created?
- One programme that you personally championed and felt proud of?
- A challenging project which you handled?
- What if you don't get this opportunity?
- Your personal growth objectives?

Keep your interviewer informed: There may be concerns and issues which can hamper your work or diminish your ability to perform effectively at time. Be sure to share it upfront. Especially, if you have any dependencies at your current firm, if you need flexibility during work hours, if there are commitments which you can't drop, or if you trade or run a business or have interests in areas that conflict with the business of the organization you are being interviewed for.

Signing off: It is a best practice to thank the interviewers, show interest in keeping in touch even if it doesn't work out. Even if you aren't taking up the offer, be clear to specify the reasons, make an attempt to keep in touch, and continue the dialogue in the future if your needs are met. You should thank people for their time, especially if senior leaders have interviewed you, seek their contact IDs to connect in the future. Be sure to acknowledge the support of the HR person who set up the interviews or the consultant who highlighted the opportunity.

In case you are taking it up: Be ready to share your plans and update them frequently on progress in coming off from your current employer. In the meantime, you can also volunteer to read up and plan for initiatives so that when you join you are ready to run with things.

PERSPECTIVE

As I waited patiently for my interview with a leader, I reflected on the posters that conveyed messages on the company's mission and core values. They visually appealed and gave me a good first-hand impression of what the organization stood for and what I could expect.

Mentally I made a note of all the possible questions I may be asked— including 'why did I want to join?', 'what was I expecting to work on?', and 'what skills did I bring to the table, especially without direct internal communications experience?'

My work folder had pieces of my editorial exploits at college. As the editor of my college environmental newsletter, *Call of the Wild*, I had revived a flagging publication. I also had the opportunity to begin and sustain a newsletter for my hostel in college apart from getting a few bylines in national newspapers while I completed my MBA. I still carry them with me to showcase the work I do as well as keep a record of my favourite campaigns. Combined with my experience in managing large accounts during my advertising stint made my case even stronger.

Later when I asked the leader about what swayed the decision to my candidature, he pointed to my proactive approach in demonstrating my skills through tangible efforts of work.

CASE STUDY

Vivek is called for an interview for an internal communications role at a leading automobile firm in the city. In the interview, he is asked to construct a questionnaire that will help the team understand the impact of a Town Hall. What must Vivek ask so that he can develop the survey?

STUDENT EXERCISE

If a firm comes on campus to select an internal communications manager, how will you go about establishing your credentials, especially without work experience? What will you list as skills and competencies that the organization is expecting?

CHAPTER 7

Crises and Internal Communications

Handling crisis communication is a vital expectation from an internal communicator. Among other expectations of internal communications, during a crisis, is to help protect the credibility of the organization, respond promptly, smooth flow of information, helping employees settle down, and get familiar. This chapter discusses in detail the role of internal communications in the time of crisis.

No crisis can be predicted, but preparedness involves commitment and diligence even when life is under control. As internal communicators, we own a large chunk of the responsibility to ensure the lines of communication are open, the relevant communicators are available, and messages are cascaded in a coordinated manner.

Managing crisis communication is a vital expectation from an internal communicator.

Among the expectations of an internal communicator during a crisis is to help protect the credibility of the organization, respond promptly, smooth flow of information, helping employees settle down, and get familiar.

In an merger and acquisition (M&A) situation, keeping the flow of information is very crucial. Other scenarios where internal communicators are invited to play a part are in change management such as job reduction, restructuring.

The CEO's weekly address with employees and daily web chat to dispel rumours and negative news articles or layoffs are effective ways to connect.

Most Employees are Seeking Information at Six Levels
1. What is the current scenario?
2. How bad is the impact?
3. What is the industry/organization doing about it?
4. What can I tell my clients/friends/family, if at all?
5. What is leadership doing to support the effort and our understanding?
6. Finally, what can I do to help out?

Framework for Articulating a Response
Often in a crisis situation, most internal communicators and leaders 'freeze' since they aren't prepared to frame suitable

responses to questions that come their way. However, there is an easy way out. You can keep the following map at the back of your mind while constructing your communication.

1. **Empathize with the situation/demonstrate care:** Remember you are addressing people who may not know the full impact of the situation. Your role as a leader or an internal communicator is to help alleviate their confusion.

2. **State facts:** Nothing but the truth. Be clear that you are calling out what you know of the issue and articulate the 5Ws (who, what, when, where, why) 1H (how).

3. **Accept what is beyond your knowledge:** Help them understand what you don't know of the issue. It is probably true that you will not know the complete picture at the start of a crisis. Remember, it isn't reflective of your capability and this is how crises are.

4. **Steps to tackle the issue:** This is very crucial since in crisis scenarios employees look to leaders to demonstrate what they are expected to do—lead the way. Explain the leadership's point of view and also what they plan to do from now till the situation is under control and after. Be honest that it is only a proposed plan.

5. **Get started and be committed:** Model the way with your action. Make the steps come alive and show your commitment.

6. **Whom do they reach out to:** Discuss who can people get more information from.

Some pointers for making internal crisis communication successful are:

- Before reporting externally, tell employees first.
- To avoid rumours, inform senior management via personal meetings.

- Choose people to inform based on their maturity levels.
- Have a formal mechanism to get feedback—questions answered on a 1:1.
- Build crisis communication team including the head of HR.
- Establish a norm that clarifies an organizational response in a stipulated time.
- Involve employees, based on crisis and understanding.
- Have consistent templates.
- Conduct mock drills to check preparedness.

Managing a Crisis

During a recent countrywide shutdown (called a bandh in India) called to protest fuel price hikes, all businesses and establishments were expected to close operations. Most IT companies decided to keep operations running due to client needs and business requirements. Employees are mostly ferried daily back and forth from their residences by transport vehicles so that they report to work on time and beat traffic. A medical transcription company's office got picketed by protesters who requested employees to go home. This unexpected turn of events took the organization by surprise; however, they managed to send their employees back home.

The unprecedented scenario met with much angst among employees on the decision to keep the office open, not getting involved in the decision, and also the actions the organization took for their safety.

To address their concerns and to ensure that employees realized how important safety was to the organization, leaders immediately crafted messages and addressed staff face-to-face the very next day. The leaders acknowledged that their decision-making wasn't the best but promised to be more cautious next time a similar scenario occurred. They took real-time feedback, noted grievances and shared plans to set up more stringent security and tracking mechanisms for overcoming crises.

This was appreciated by people who saw leaders as credible, honest, and transparent.

A communication plan with a clear line of action involved employees at all levels to know if the measures indeed made sense.

Case Study: Waterlogging and Addressing Safety Concerns

Here is another case study on how internal communications plays an important role in overcoming crises and mitigating staff's concerns.

When torrential downpours across Delhi crippled traffic, upset transport fleet management, and inconvenienced a lot of transport users, it was a recipe for an internal PR disaster.

The leadership was quick to acknowledge the concerns people had about leveraging available resources; it focused on the positive steps the organization took to alleviate the issues that cropped up. Such as the effort transport staffers took to support people who were stranded, communication modes used, and measures taken to make the journey to their destinations comfortable. The leaders also looked at best practices from how other organizations manage their fleets and people in trying conditions and recommended steps they would take going forward. More face-to-face communication via Town Halls and emphasis on safety of people helped overcome negative vibes that emerged from this crisis. However, leaders also emphasized the role of people in ensuring resources were best utilized by urging flexibility and openness to solutions offered by the transport team. It was a win-win situation that was shared. The communication that staff received got great feedback. In fact, one employee wrote back stating how impressed she was with the effort taken by the transport staff. Also how secure she felt working for an organization that took measures for women's safety. Another mentioned that the approach of acknowledging mistakes and providing measures to overcome them made him feel that the organization truly made an effort.

Case Study: 2010 Delhi Commonwealth Games

In this case, I discuss how business continuity planning can support crisis mitigation.

The Games (3–14October) was slated as the biggest multisport event conducted in India so far. With over 70 countries fielding teams and 3,400 sports persons and 12,000 delegates participating, there were always going to be potential hurdles with employee availability, transport, accommodation, road passage, and travel plans.

So even if you didn't have an office in Delhi, there could have been impact to work—with keeping clients informed, employees commuting to and from office, stakeholders transiting the country, or someone needing visas to travel among others.

To begin, a core team comprising leadership and internal groups (office administration, internal communications, HR, among others) discussed potential concerns and challenges that the Games could throw.

A comprehensive business continuity and communication plan ensured that we shared updates with key stakeholders, anticipated scenarios, and potential costs.

Experience matters: While employees knew that the organization had little control over what happened during the Games and the condition of the roads, they expected to be involved and kept abreast of positive steps taken to improve their overall experience during that period. A central helpdesk allowed employees to seek clarifications on transport and potential issues that could crop up. Leaders were nominated to front end any direct conversations and listed key contacts on the intranet.

Crowdsourcing—a game changer: By inviting employees to play the 'eyes and ears' of the organization, it helped plan business contingencies better. For example, employees sent in presentations and other material they sourced from the web, pointing to impacted roads and other scenarios that the organization didn't anticipate earlier. An employee who enrolled as a volunteer with the Commonwealth Games (CWG) team had insights on areas to avoid during the event. Similarly, employees were asked to define what time worked best for them so that they could plan their work better and keep their stakeholders informed.

Better safe than sorry: By deciding to shutter the office during the Games' closing ceremony and work on an alternate day, the organization took no chances with enough warnings of chaos and increased security measures. It turned out that this was the right move—we heard about 75,000 people attended the finale.

Travel with discretion: Even though visitors and clients came during the fortnight, expectations were set on what they could see in the city and the inconvenience that they might face. There were questions on terror threats and if the event would finally get held apart from the news on corruption. Travellers were pointed to the CWG website, the internal intranet page, and travel guidance for their clarifications. Advisories were published periodically so that all travellers were on the same page.

Transport blues: Most companies anticipated fewer cabs and even lesser drivers since most were going to be engaged during the Games. The organization pre-empted this by ensuring the eventuality of more vehicles, rescheduled pick-up and drops, leveraged the Metro, and encouraged employees to car pool.

Saving for a rainy day: Organizations stocked up dry food, fuel for generators, pre-booked guest houses in case of stay-overs, and invested in backups for the premises. Clients and partners were informed of our plans and kept in the loop of changes. Laptops were provided to teams with critical needs.

Engaging employees with internal communications: Internal communications had a pivotal role to play in this exercise. Employees and leaders were requested to share updates with stakeholders, think of options to work from home if possible, retain key emergency numbers, and ensure team members were equipped with spare laptops to tide over any eventuality. They were encouraged to carry their car papers and identification cards in case of security checks on Delhi roads.

Answering pertinent questions: Not surprisingly, employees had many questions about safety, their role in the process, next steps in an emergency, and if they could work from home. By articulating these as consistent messages and cascading it through, leaders allowed meaningful conversations and timely information sharing.

Crisis situations are welcome at times: This specific event gave us the opportunity to rally employees together, to work collaboratively, update their contact information (we had challenges with employees keeping their profiles current), and building rigour into business continuity planning.

Case Study: Chile Miners Rescue

This rescue captured the interest of the world and incidentally is among the world's most successful operations to get miners out from the longest underground entrapment in history. The meticulous planning, the pace at which the government moved to locate the group, get help when needed, include necessary safeguards, keep their families united above ground, and the media informed, all showcased the key role of communication, both internal and external.

Here are some of the elements of the entire operation that got me thinking in relation to internal communications within organizations.

During the first few days while efforts were on to establish if the miners could be rescued or not, the country promptly took steps to gain the confidence of their people by sacking those responsible for the mine's safety. The first step after establishing contact was to send in supplies to get their digestive systems functioning before sharing solid food. Rescue teams also sent oxygen down to where they were trapped. *To me, establishing the 'basics' is crucial for stability and giving employees confidence in the ability of their leaders and organizations.*

With limited resources and technology infrastructure, Chile reached out to National Aeronautics and Space Administration (NASA) for help and sought support of their satellites and experts. The NASA sent its team to consult on the rescue mission but also got involved in supporting how the miners were treated and looked after (based on their experiences with space station astronauts). Experts from the Chile Navy were called in to help design the rescue capsule. *Establishing the right team and equipping them with the right tools enables consistent communication and accurate results.*

A communications system was installed through which each of the men spoke and reported their feeling to doctors and psychologists on the top. Then a systematic plan was created to keep the miners informed and busy. According to media reports, NASA experts were invited to share their expertise of helping people cope with long periods of solitude.

A conscious effort made to build trust by sharing appropriate news and set expectations ensured the miners were all on the same page. The miners were kept occupied with games and were made to get into a routine so that time was broken into chunks. The rescue team also reviewed communication that was exchanged between families and miners below so that wrong messages weren't communicated. *Building robust internal communications networks is essential to keeping employees focused on the goals; in this case, coming out safely and getting united with their families.*

They also thought of ways to involve them in problem solving and plan for how they would cope after they came up to the surface, since there were fears of information overload and from separation from the real world. They were also instructed to wear eye shades so as to avoid vision concerns when they get rescued. Besides their immediate physical needs, the team above ground prepared psychiatric counselling for all miners. To begin, they helped the group establish a leader with the help of a questionnaire. *Involving and empowering employees during a crisis and getting them to chart their own success are crucial for organizational alignment.*

There were rumours of the forming of splinter groups frustrated by the delayed operations and periodic communication (through videos, photos, notes, and even watching a soccer match!) and a seasoned leader (their foreman) kept them on track. *Established leadership code of conduct to ensure communication flows smoothly and employees know how to focus on the end outcome.*

Finally, it was phenomenal to see how the president of the country personally oversaw the operation with the mining minister and greeted each miner as they emerged to share messages for their families. Not sure how many other countries came as much for their people. This example reinforced the message. October 13, the day they were all rescued, is also now a permanent holiday in Chile. Rallying a country just on hope is itself awe inspiring.

When Not to Communicate

Very often in a crisis, most leaders sway between communicating excessively or not communicating at all. Mostly, the easiest way to get a message out is an email, but it does have implications. Both extremes aren't a safe bet when it comes to crises. Employees expect to know from leaders on the issues and the organization's perspective sooner than later. In fact, delaying any communication only results in rumour mills taking over.

However, there are times when the appropriate channels of communication need to route the messages for information to be assimilated accurately.

Take, for instance, Rajesh, a business head of a medium-sized IT services firm who intervened when an employee began abusing and manhandling support staff due to an altercation. This employee had to be physically removed from the premises and a code of conduct violation served to him. However, those who witnessed the episode on the floor (the organization occupied multiple floors in an IT park in the city) expected an explanation and the next steps from the incident.

Rajesh planned to send out an email to the entire office, thinking that the word had gone to everyone. I polled a few employees from all floors and realized that an email may cause panic rather than support their understanding. I recommended that he set up an informal meeting with staff on the floor where the incident took place and take questions. That strategy worked and staff received Rajesh's approach well—of proactively addressing the issue with them directly.

CASE STUDY

Toyo, a mobile phone company, recalls over 50 million pieces of its XT-5 battery since they are prone to bursting when overcharged.

Create messages to inform the media and get employees on your side.

Define steps to overcome the situation before it becomes a black mark against your company's reputation.

STUDENT EXERCISE

A hoax mail reached employees in your organization telling them of an upcoming lay-off. The word is spreading fast across all levels of the company and it is causing panic. As an internal communicator, who is tasked with stemming this crisis and what will be your plan of action?

- How can you help alleviate the fears among staff?
- What will you do to ensure leaders are equipped to handle the situation?

CHAPTER 8

The Future of Internal Communications

There is a shift in the way internal communications is taking place. To raise their game, internal communicators have to build a strong business case and demonstrate value over time. The future of internal communications is discussed in detail in this chapter.

As organizations grapple with issues such as engagement, attrition, and social media adoption, the role of internal communications gets more and more prominent. Internal communication as a function will be more active in driving and managing change, engaging staff, and influencing how organizations drive business results. This chapter looks at insights, trends, and results from India's first internal communications study.

There is a shift in the way internal communications is taking place. With more and more organizations debating the impact and implications of Web 2.0 on their staff, the internal communicator is expected to serve as a consultant in distilling trends and recommending relevant solutions for integration, knowledge management, and learning.

Also with increased targeted 'internal' marketing to career levels, such as the key 'manager' community, internal communications will need to structure direct messages and manage its internal constituents better. The internal communicator will need to be seen more and more as a 'people' integrator who can construct a 360-degree plan that supports the employees' life cycle of the organization from the on-boarding to the alumni stages.

In the next five years, there will be an increase in the demand for specialists in internal communications and strategic consultants who can leverage evolving trends in employee communications.

That said, it expects internal communicators to 'let go' of control of content and empower employees to co-create communication.

It will also mean that internal communicators need to build a network of champions who will be the eyes and ears on the ground. The role will evolve to that of an oversight function and less of an administrative group. According to the 2010 'Trends in Internal Communications' report (Edelman, 2010a), employees will be the organization's next new product. There will be greater emphasis on conversations driving decisions and managers will hardly have a role considering how much information is available for employees to glean from other sources. The leaders' role will evolve to one that rallies rather than prescribes direction. Careers as an expectation will see a dramatic shift as employees develop their self-identity from what they do rather than which organization they belong to.

Interestingly, increased intranet usage, corporate identity, and change management are seen as the future. Internal communicators believe increased efficiency and information overload to be focus areas while strongly accepting the importance of internal communication. Many are confident that headcounts and budgets will go up (European Federation of Internal Communication Association, 2009).

The Trends in Internal Communications

Internal communicators will be front and centre of change: Change management will become an essential component of an internal communicator, and their expertise will be sought more often. Their scope and expectation will range from organization design to leadership succession planning.

Talent management and retention will draw even more on the power of internal communication: attrition is looming as a challenge for organizations, especially in India. Unlike earlier, compensation isn't going to be the reason for employees shifting companies. Among the key drivers are avenues for growth, opportunities to learn, options to accumulate wealth, get to work on challenging projects, and receive real-time recognition. Internal communications, therefore, will play an integral role in keeping employees aligned and focused on the organization's goals while emphasizing staff's role in the journey.

Tapping internal talent for improved engagement: Harvesting internal talent for internal communications is the way forward to manage speedier communication, improve engagement, garner acceptance as well as keep budgets in control. I foresee it leading to lesser dependence on professional agencies and communication outfits. Very often, we underestimate the power of what our employees can visualize and create. Co-creation of content and publishing will improve how internal communication is perceived and conducted. The more you involve your employees, the greater the chances of acceptance. The key to successful leadership communication and employee engagement is reverse mentoring. Unless leaders take time to learn first-hand from 'next Gen', they will always feel inadequate and unsure of their efforts.

Social activism and transparency: Employees will continue to seek even greater transparency and trust as boundaries defining organizations blur with social media access and adoption. In this world of 'Wikileaks', internal communicators must be able to acknowledge that any communication shared internally may find its way out. Social activism is on the rise and unless employers understand and listen intently to their staff, they will continue to be surprised when internal literature leaks out or specific company policies are discussed or appear on social networking sites. Internal communicators have the onus of closely monitoring staff's participation in social media to gain insights and feedback on what isn't probably getting shared in-house. All this without encroaching on their privacy. Understanding and converging energies internally to align with corporate goals will be a key priority.

Internal communications consulting for department and unit levels: Employee engagement continues to be an issue with businesses emerging from the recent downturn. Managing engagement at the organization level will lose traction as employees continue to demonstrate closer connection and commitment to their immediate circle of peers and supervisors. Each unit lead will hold immense clout over how aligned the employee in his team is vis-à-vis the firm. Internal communicators will be sought after as consultants to draw out strategies at the micro level as well as provide resources to 'plug and play'.

Your employee is your internal conduit: Viewing each individual in the organization as a potential internal communications conduit will be an important mind shift internal communicators will need to make. Staff's immense clout to add context and value to internal communications is currently underutilized. I believe audio and video usage will see a spurt with better technologies, mobile devices, and increased bandwidth ensuring information sharing is seamless and faster. Empowering employees to contribute and manage internal communication channels and flow will see an uptick in progressive firms.

Internal communicators as marketing professionals: Convergence of internal and external communication will further break down boundaries and responsibilities. It will mean increased collaboration on projects, enhanced transparency, and division of work for a consolidated brand experience. At times, internal communicators will need to lead more to ensure maximum value of campaigns and promotions. This could mean having a greater understanding of marketing tricks and tools that can be internally leveraged.

Specialists sought: I foresee increased specialization within the internal communications function with professionals expected to lead cross-cultural communication, manage diversity, engage in crisis management, practise storytelling, build a social organization, partner for change, and drive communication leadership. What works in one country or region can now be replicated easily with a deep understanding of culture and local needs. Internal communicators will be sought after as cross-cultural ambassadors due to their access to leadership, information, and the ability to influence engagement.

Internal communicators as thought leaders: Internal communicators need to create opportunities for their role and get to the table as thought leaders. Getting a seat at the table has a lot to do with demonstrating consistent value, building credibility, and being a thought leader. Respect for the role comes with increased knowledge of how internal communicators effectively partner with stakeholders to improve information reach, access, and sharing. Contributing thought leadership beyond the organization will be an expectation from internal communicators.

Internal communication and employer branding: Building an employer brand will witness greater involvement by internal communicators to craft suitable messages and bring relevant practices for making the organization an employer of choice. Employer branding will extend into recruitment marketing, induction programmes, corporate branding, and alumni connection to provide a holistic employee experience.

Managing personal brands and personalities within the organizational context: As organizations become more connected and social, employees will look to coexist their personal brands in the real world and online with their personalities within firms.

There is a huge opportunity to tap the power of employees' personal equity for brand building as well as spreading the good word about the organization's internal practices.

State of the Nation: 2011 Internal Communications India Survey Results

The State of the Nation: 2011 Internal Communications India Survey (Verghese, 2011) was carried out between September and October 2011. Communication practitioners in India were invited to participate in this first ever study aimed at gauging the value and impact of internal communications. Respondents who completed the survey were professionals based in India who work or have worked for organizations either in the capacity of a leader or an individual contributor in the internal communications function. Twenty-five practitioners from industries such as pharmaceutical, IT, banking, energy, telecom, and health participated in the study with a majority of them from organizations over 3,000 employees.

The survey covered the following themes:

- Background and Role
- The Internal Communicator's Profile
- Internal Communications Team Construct
- Planning and Skills
- Focus Areas
- Expectations of the Function
- Return of Investment
- Channels
- Measurement
- Leadership Support for Internal Communications
- Executive Communications

- Challenges Faced by the Function
- Social Media and Internal Communications
- The Future of Internal Communications

This survey sought insights from practitioners on the function's state of affairs, get feedback on the impact they make in their role, company and industry, how leaders and communicators guide decisions, and raise the level of the function in the country.

Respondents who completed the survey received a free executive summary of the results and were invited for further discussion on the subject in the future.

KEY FINDINGS

- The understanding of internal communications is limited in the country, and there is scope for training and education.
- Only half of internal communications accepted that they were aware of skills and expertise to do internal communications. Employee engagement, crafting messages, designing, and implementing communication were among the top-ranked responsibilities that internal communicators owned.
- Very few (36 per cent) had a clear understanding of their role as an internal communicator and admitted to not getting recognition for their work. Stakeholders had limited understanding of internal communications strategy and the plan created by communicators.
- Less than half of the respondents mentioned they had internal communications budgets to run their function. Most funds were centrally allocated from HQ of their respective companies and they had limited control on how it got distributed.
- Only a third agreed that leadership bought-in to internal communications and less than half were confident of pitching a business case for internal communications.

- Less than a third of respondents had their internal communications objectives aligned with their company's goals.
- The top three focus areas at work for internal communicators were employee engagement, translating leadership messages, and channel management.
- Internal communicators had differing viewpoints on the definition, objectives, and outcomes expected from the function. Most understood it as strategic in nature, important for the organization, relevant to conducting two-way communication, crucial to building pride, and needed to engage stakeholders for meeting organizational objectives.
- Channels mostly used by internal communicators in India included email, face-to-face, intranet, print publications, posters, TVs, surveys, and video. Strangely, social media as a channel didn't register among respondents as vital. According to respondents, the most effective channels were email, Town Halls (read face-to-face communication), and intranet.
- Awareness of internal communications measurement was low among respondents, and only 11 per cent accepted they knew how to measure the output of their work. A majority of communicators said they measured their work quarterly (35 per cent) and real-time (23 per cent). Mostly measurement was directed at 'message assimilation and understanding' (25 per cent), employee reach (17 per cent), and behaviour change (11 per cent).
- Only 50 per cent felt they were well supported by their leadership, and only 37 per cent agreed completely that their leaders believed in the impact of internal communications on the organization.
- Social media is yet to find a place in internal communications. Six per cent of respondents admitted to having a business case for social media adoption in internal

communications, although 50 per cent had invested in building social media inside the organization and 56 per cent had a policy in place.

Internal communicators in India need to take the initiative: There seemed to be a lack of initiative with communicators to engage leaders in a dialogue and also in their ability to present newer and better ways to communicate. Less than a third had conversations on internal communications and only 25 per cent got the opportunity to discuss newer forms of effective communications. Respect for the function, micromanaging, and overwhelming work were barriers cited for not committing time on these fronts.

Understanding of impact and value internal communication limited: Internal communicators weren't able to consistently state how and what value and impact the function contributed to. Among the key themes that emerged were a need to 'create a sense of ownership and engagement within the organization', 'form, educate, engage and energize', 'build a strong employer brand', and 'build loyalty and belonging towards the company'. The range of responses indicated the need for consistency amongst professionals. Respondents shared the need for ROI, building engagement, improving employees' performance, engaging and building communities, being an employer of choice, and taking feedback as among the top outcomes. Interestingly, a few mentioned the need for 'happy' workforces, thereby, indicating the role of internal communications in relation to the well-being of staff.

Lack of motivation hampers interest and outcomes: Overall, only 52 per cent of those polled felt they were motivated enough to give their best to internal communications. Half the internal communicators surveyed felt they were well supported by their leadership, and only 37 per cent agreed completely that their leaders believed in the impact of internal communications on the organization.

More interventions needed to raise the game with executive communication: When asked to gauge the range and maturity of leadership communication, a low percentage (25 per cent) agreed that leaders were effective in communicating with staff, although communicators did feel supported in empowering leaders with material. There is growing interest in leveraging communication but without enough staff to pull their weight, communicators aren't able to deliver up to expectations. One respondent put it plainly—'They would have liked me to do a lot more especially with each of the BU heads, but we were short on strength. Being geographically spread had its own challenges.' There is a need to get leaders to communicate more frequently and pay attention to increasing two-way interaction.

Future of Internal Communications Looks Promising

Internal communicators believe that organizations today primarily grapple with managing employee expectations, building employer branding, and managing change. In the future, they hope to be able to contribute significantly to managing change, engaging staff, and integrating social media.

Social media stood out as the most significant trend in the future. The emergence of social media as a key tool for internal communication, social media expansion, and internal networking were enough reason to believe that this trend would be front and centre of what internal communicators focused on in the years to come.

EVOLUTION OF THE ROLE

Communicators didn't seem very sure of how their role would evolve in the future (30 per cent agreeing completely to the question), and only 46 per cent believed internal communications had a future in their organization. The skills they believe would be most crucial for the role were:

* Multitasking abilities
* Communication
* Time management
* Understanding technology
* Business knowledge
* Influencing
* 'Human' touch
* Social media
* Translating messages
* Pulse of the organization
* Programme management
* Change management

To make an impact in the future, internal communicators felt they needed to do a lot more. Here are some broad recommendations.

* Ability to work smoothly across geographies and divisions
* Raise their level of influence
* Flexible and versatile
* Listen more
* Network better
* Get involved early in planning
* Demonstrate value
* Treat each need uniquely
* Create more visibility for function

Conclusion

The internal communications function in India is quite nascent, and while there is growing interest among leaders and organizations to do more, lack of awareness and resources are limiting progress. To raise their game, internal communicators have to build a strong business case and demonstrate value over time. Significant investments in training and development of professionals and leadership attention are crucial for the success of this function. Internal communicators have a role to play by building skills, understanding business challenges, sharing best practices, and investing time to improve leaders' understanding of the impact internal communications can make. There is potential for this profession in India as the country's economy grows.

CASE STUDY

Aziz, 22, joined Connect Wiz, a global telecom provider as an associate from campus. In his first interaction with his CEO, he bluntly posed the question on why the firm wasn't investing enough in patents and Research and Development (R&D) much to the embarrassment of his team's project manager. Aziz wants to be involved in decisions that are impacting the organization's growth since he believes he has a stake in the process. How can his project manager and the CEO be coached on engaging staff such as Aziz and put the company's plans in perspective with their wants, needs, and expectations?

STUDENT EXERCISE

With the future of internal communications to be defined by how employees participate in the process and distribution, you are invited by your CEO to craft a programme to involve staff to celebrate your organization's 50th founding day. Devise plans to support staff's understanding of the event, celebrate the successes and lessons from history, and excite future prospects to join the company.

CHAPTER 9

Employee Engagement and Inclusive Internal Communications

The employee's commitment to the organization and motivation is crucial to the organization's success. The challenges faced by organizations these days include attrition, communication, career development, and engagement— while trying to keep pace with explosive economic growth. In such a scenario, internal communicators need to articulate a vision and culture to keep the workforce motivated and energized.

In this chapter we focus on getting employees included in internal communications. The challenges and the opportunities ahead are manifold and we discuss how to consider higher employee expectations to stay on top of their game.

Employee Engagement and Inclusive Internal Communications

The Indian IT-BPO industry continues to be the source of employment for people across the nation. According to National Association of Software and Services Companies (NASSCOM), India's leading industry body organizations are expected to empower staff with improved skills—foreign language capabilities, global business process knowledge, sales and marketing skills, research (business, market, financial), and business analytics. India, with its strengths in the form of low-cost manpower, a large pool of skilled, English-speaking workforce, and government support, is emerging as a preferred destination for outsourced services. India's talent pool is expanding rapidly with 4.4 million graduates and postgraduates in 2011–2012 (NASSCOM, 2009). Internally, organizations are taking several employee engagement initiatives to retain staff including retention/performance-based bonuses, rewards and recognitions, career development programmes, and involving them in Corporate Social Responsibility (CSR) initiatives (NASSCOM, 2012).

A large portion of India's population is between the age of 15 and 59, and more than half below the age of 25. Work is done using the most suitable blend of locations in the fastest and most cost-effective way possible—sophisticatedly called 'blended' or 'outsourced' delivery. This concept also employs the 'shared service centre' model where one location services multiple geographies and customers at the same time, thereby improving utilization.

Engaging Employees Isn't Easy

In this scenario, all outsourcing locations are ideally supposed to be closely integrated in terms of processes, brand values, and messaging. Effective communication holds the key. In fact, research indicates that companies that communicate effectively are 4.5 times more likely to report high levels of employee engagement versus firms that communicate less effectively. Companies that are highly effective communicators are 20 per cent more likely to report lower turnover rates than their peers (Watson Wyatt, 2006).

India has a lot to cheer about! The recent WorkAsia research study completed by Watson Wyatt (2008a) indicates that India has the highest percentage of highly engaged workers in Asia at 78 per cent, whilst Japan has the lowest employee engagement level at 39 per cent. Head to head with China, the engagement level of the Indian worker is 20 per cent more than his/her Chinese counterpart.

These are all encouraging signs—but the challenges and the opportunities ahead are manifold. The imminent US slowdown, shrinking talent pool, slowdown in hiring, and higher employee expectations are reason enough for internal communicators to stay on top of their game.

The challenges faced by organizations in India are around attrition, communication, career development, and engagement—while trying to keep pace with explosive economic growth. The BPO outfits experience the highest attrition rates, losing staff at a rate of between 100 per cent and 200 per cent a year. It is widely believed that organizations spend an average of 36 per cent of their revenues on their employees but do not have a tangible way to measure its impact.

A Mercer's (2008) study—'What's Working'—is made up of a series of national research on worker insights, highlighting factors that make a difference to employee engagement. The survey's 125 questions elicit views in the areas defined by Mercer's Human Capital Strategy Model and cover training and development, work environment, leadership, performance management, work-life balance, communication, compensation, benefits, and engagement.

The India study throws up some fascinating directions for HR and internal communications professionals.

Employee engagement is no longer just about the employee's intent to leave. The employee's commitment to the organization and motivation to contribute to the organization's success plays a significant role. The top three drivers in India are trust in senior management, how the organization is perceived for customer service, and fair pay. Surprisingly, from an India context, the least valued factors in the continuum were benefits, compensation, and performance management.

In India, having a long-term career is considered positive and stable. Frequent job changes are viewed negatively and therefore the high scores around the commitment count are in line with this common mindset.

Internal communications and HR professionals need to take note of the employee's need for giving feedback and to observe subsequent action. The study reveals that employees seem to be getting very little information on their organization's vision and future plans, a cause for concern.

Other areas which require action include the organization's reputation in the market—congruent to other research in this space, which believes that organizations that are socially responsible are considered better places to work.

In the talent management bracket, managers fare poorly for their levels of involvement, understanding, and support as well as for merit-based appraisals.

In India, with a large number of global players entering the market, the talent pool now has a plethora of choices and even these multinationals are finding it tough to retain staff. Softer styles of leadership have a better impact in India and China, leaving organizations to develop or seek leaders who can fill this need.

Some more reports probe employee engagement deeper and provide good pointers to communicators.

Watson Wyatt's (2008b) report on global work attitudes indicates that customer focus is a key driver of employee engagement across all regions, while the main drivers of employee engagement are similar around the world: effective communication, competitive compensation and benefits, a clear customer focus and confidence in the strategic direction, and leadership of the organization. It is important to note that the employee perceptions of these key drivers vary too. Compensation and benefits and communication fared poorly.

A research by Kenexa (2007) suggests that an organization's active participation in corporate social responsibility efforts has a significant influence on employees' engagement levels and views of senior management.

It is interesting to note the common threads among the 15 best companies to work for in India (*Business World*, 2007) included opportunities for interesting work, challenging targets, and growth and development. Compensation wasn't a top factor, which served as a relief for organizations facing challenges with sky rocketing salaries.

This is corroborated by the Best Employers in Asia 2007 study (Hewitt Associates, 2007) in partnership with The Wall Street Journal Asia. In India, career opportunities are considered a top priority for a restless and ambitious workforce. The message is clear—organizations that are able to manage employees' career aspirations will have a more connected workforce.

The Indian connection with engagement is outlined in the Power and the Glory, a J. Walter Thomson (JWT) Brand Chakras study discussed in the blog Coffee and Donuts with JWT Planning. This talks of the four areas which Indians have in their ethos—work as a channel for creativity and accomplishment, name for themselves, image, and ability to give back to society. Indians tend to idolize leaders and this study says that the younger generation is keen to use their talents to get a seat at the main table (JWT, 2007).

Deloitte's study (2008) on talent engagement shows a widening gap in employee commitment across the globe. The research bases itself on the premise that the contest for human capital is evident everywhere, although the nature and significance of trends vary from country to country. Only those companies that win the hearts and minds of their top talent will be able to deliver value over both the short and long terms.

Whilst I firmly believe that India's cultural and economic shifts impact the way jobs and careers are viewed, the onus on engagement is a big responsibility for managers. Buckingham and Coffman (1999) succinctly describe this notion.

Communication is a vital element in energizing a flagging workforce. The research points to overcoming information overload. Getting employees to manage their work and performance by providing them with the necessary tools is another way to motivate and engage.

The research proposes a model—Develop, Deploy, Connect—taking into account alignment, capability, performance, and commitment. I personally feel the toughest element in the model to implement is the Connect component. Connecting calls for greater transparency and trust, which employees must perceive. The model talks of connecting like improving the quality of interactions and building networks—both essential elements of a social media perspective. So, does it mean social media efforts internally help build greater engagement?

These pointers are crucial for internal communicators—to remodel the way communication needs to get created, shared, and viewed. Social media tools will play a defining role in building trust and transparency, driving engagement, and helping measure the impact of how employees view their employers.

There are also a few firms in India which have taken employee feedback and recommendations from consultants seriously. Helping employees understand their role in the organization's growth, channelling creative energies, and allowing freedom at work have delivered results to these organizations. Internal communications programmes which link back to the brand are methods adopted by forward thinking organizations.

Reality, however, is different and a few questions persist: do companies manage to engage employees in their outsourced arms as much as they do at the parent divisions?

Sense of Remoteness

The challenge is to work towards a 'one' global company. Furthermore, the work assigned may not be client-facing when it comes to delivering technology solutions and services. There is a front-ending client team which routes work to India and other such locations. This buffering creates a sense of remoteness, which perhaps gets translated into the working style.

It is important to also understand the business context in which outsourced organizations exist—if they are listed, there is a greater degree of accountability and transparency while it may not hold good for a privately held firm.

With companies racing to get business and the best people, the importance of communication is often ignored. There are a few probable reasons for this lack of commitment.

Last in the Queue

To begin, it may be a factor of the model itself. Outsourced assignments are typically considered as 'back-end' tasks. Companies are often ignorant of the impact of effective communication on business efficiency. Communication with employees in outsourced locations is therefore considered optional.

The other reason is the changing perception of the outsourcing industry. Many are trying to shed the 'low-cost' tag attached with work done in India and develop the 'brand' and 'quality' angles. Home-grown companies such as Infosys and Wipro have scripted strong 'Made in India' stories taking global giants head-on.

However, a few global corporations continue to underestimate the scale and scope of operations. India is a large and culturally diverse nation and most companies prefer to spread operations across the key cities and hubs based on demand and client needs. With this comes the need to engage employees, personalize information, and integrate communication routes.

So, does this call for companies to look at communication differently with their outsourced arms?

Multilayered Cascades

Typically, companies employ leadership communication in the form of 'state of the business notes', which get directly relayed or cascaded to employees. Specific local messages are often conveyed by the leadership through employee forums or newsletters. On the third level, there are the delivery network communiqués that integrate global teams and enable sharing of best practices.

Most organizations have robust intranets and portals with the maturity to handle collaboration tools and systems, thereby increasing transparency and smooth flow of information. Based on the priorities and internal structures, organizations relay information via locations geographically located near the delivery centres—for example, if a centre is based at Mauritius, the India location, either a sales or a marketing division takes the lead to oversee communication and integration.

Culture and Communication

Discussions with my peers in the industry have led me to believe that culture plays a vital role in communication with regard to India.

In their quest to maintain the balance of a 'global network', most companies fail to take on board the localization factors such as using Asian faces and imagery in their communication, localized words that the audience can easily relate to. In fact, there are lessons to be learnt from McDonalds and Pizza Hut that have customized their menu to suit Indian palates. But then there are downsides to this approach as well. I was regaled with an anecdote—of a cricketing analogy used by the CEO of an MNC to convey a business success, which was not understood by associates in other parts of the globe where the game was not played or understood. It took quick thinking on the part of a senior executive to play a recorded version of a cricket match to the uninformed!

PERSPECTIVE

In my opinion, while it may be easy to transfer jobs to another location, integrating employees and helping them imbibe the culture of an organization may take longer. Change can only be brought about by actively localizing behaviours which then get communicated. I quizzed some of my counterparts in IT firms with outsourced work in India and the findings across the board were the same.

India is a different ball game and companies are realizing why it makes immense sense to send their global executives to get acclimatized. There are today, a large number of expatriates working in India and China to get 'closer to the action'. The challenges in getting employees on the same page when it comes to branding are a factor of a few aspects like culture and diversity along with communication. The scale of operations, large workforces, and diverse locations—all make the equation harder to manage. Some companies have workforces in India numbering over 30,000 in the country.

In fact, a large Indian IT firm harps on this aspect of outsourcing in its pitch against its competitors. I remember reading a recruitment advertisement which talked of making a choice between a global Indian firm and that of a far-flung arm of an inter-galactic wing of a global company!

Opportunities beyond Dreams

So, does moving work to India mean a lot to those employed in India?

It certainly does—for a youngster just out of college, landing a job in an MNC is a dream come true. In India, the bigger the brand name, the better are the opportunities for the individual's growth. A generation older cannot dream of the opportunities their children today chase.

India incidentally has the largest English-speaking talent pool in the world. Three-fifths of the Indian technical workforce has more than four years of experience and an even higher proportion has an engineering degree. This is an excellent plus point for regulating the constant flow of work to India.

Moving work to India is not regarded as making jobs redundant elsewhere but instead seen as an opportunity to do 'more for less'—that is, provide more value for the same spend.

The opportunity to work on projects for large, global clients apart from learning new technologies is a huge attraction for these knowledge workers. Also, Indian operations have moved up the value chain to handle complex, high-end work as opposed to maintenance engagements done in most other regions.

So, how can companies communicate better and get employees to feel part of the global network? Here are a few recommendations to get started:

Invest in creating an employee brand: To start with, there needs to be consistency in brand and internal communications messaging across the organization irrespective of location. All employees need to be inducted formally and made to follow these in letter and spirit. To be successful, an organization cannot afford a 'remote' part of any team. In fact, onshore, near shore, and offshore teams need to work together to achieve the delivery targets. A substantial investment in building brand ambassadors of employees is imperative if the industry wishes to tame the challenge of attrition. Attrition levels range from 15 per cent to 60 pe cent per year among ITeS companies. The average attrition level for a voice-based call centre is 40 per cent. This presents huge challenges in workforce management. There is a certain amount of hype associated with working in an ITeS environment. Many professionals leave the industry finding the monotonous nature of the work overbearing, and working in night shifts physically exhausting. It is critical for organizations to help these professionals understand the requirement and expectations.

Brand reinforcement and training are essential: The key reason for the high turnover can be attributed to training ineffectiveness and faulty recruitment processes. There are some glaring examples which made news recently of poor referral checks resulting in a wrong fit. Formal brand training and reinforcement refreshers on a periodic basis are a must. Having senior leadership talk informally with employees is a big boost to their morale and helps set a context to organizational direction. However, once employees have got through the initial period and become leaders of the organizational process, they should be engaged as mentors. I would strongly recommend training on cultural sensitivities even if the employee is not closely associated with client-facing interactions.

Empower local communicators: Companies should build and empower local communications teams that have an understanding of what 'ticks'. For example, companies tend to hand down communication created at headquarters which is far removed from local realities. Sometimes creating templates do not work in such scenarios. Organizations have revised their internal programmes with India-specific messages around growth, opportunities, work–life balance, and job satisfaction among others. One large multinational decided to revisit their global recruitment campaign to build a 'first in kind' India story with separate messages for the audience in the country.

Articulate the future clearly: There is always a sense of un-easiness when it comes to working with multinationals based on earlier experiences the country has faced. The 'hire and fire' methods employed by firms have been resented in a country where government-run units ensured security with pensions and union engagement. Questions are asked about the future in terms of the organization's commitment and business stability. Companies need to articulate a vision and culture to keep the workforce motivated and energized. Be transparent and honest in your communication. There is no greater loss than an organization caught for hiding information from its own employees.

Increase communication engagement leveraging new media: Communicating face-to-face with employees is becoming extremely difficult, considering the tremendous spurt in headcount ramp-up. Usage of collaborative tools like webcasts, IM, virtual tours, discussion boards, and leadership blogs should be explored to increase two-way communication and get a pulse of employees. Some organizations are cagey about using these tools considering the risks that they highlight; there are numerous success stories as well.

Expose local communication teams to global best practices: By encouraging local communication teams to visit headquarters and exposing them to global best practices, they will be able to understand business objectives and incorporate elements to a local context. Also promote communicators for workshops and conferences on various communication subjects. This helps in retaining the flavour of the best practices while making it relevant locally.

So while companies continue their outsourcing partnerships in the region, there is a greater need to focus on communicating effectively. '

Here are some recommendations on how internal communicators can improve the dialogue and create a sustained impact with their communication.

1. Focus on aligning your local message and branding with your company's global image, clearly revealing why employees should join your organization.
2. Work with HR to identify and build opportunities for greater employee engagement, which go beyond the workplace and include the local community.
3. Emphasize the importance of fair practice and a meritocracy in your communication, thereby expanding employee understanding of how they contribute towards your company's bottom line.
4. In India, the family is an individual's centre. Some organizations have learnt to involve parents and other stakeholders during the employee life cycle to improve engagement. Internal communicators can focus on this angle of the employee's life a bit more to further drive engagement.

CASE STUDY

Ravi, an internal communications manager at Global Pix, an Indian firm with operations in over 20 cities in the country, has been asked to recommend a strategy to align and integrate employees from Prompt TV, a large digital media agency with over 50 offices globally that his organization recently acquired. Considering this is the first such acquisition that his firm is doing, he is keen to ensure the merger is successful and employees from the acquired agency feel part of the Global Pix family. What steps should he take to retain staff, improve morale, and drive engagement?

STUDENT EXERCISE

Read the recent best places to work/great place to work studies and list internal communications strategies by organizations to engage staff.

CHAPTER 10

Integrating Social Media with Internal Communications: Challenges and Opportunities

Social media is becoming a preferred medium for sharing knowledge and experiences. The options available for communicators have exponentially expanded and the advantages of social media for internal communications are numerous and evident. Those successfully implementing social media have taken the time to absorb the various elements surrounding this phenomenon and create effective policies and guidelines to build long-term relationships with the employees.

Social media in India has come a long way in the last five years and it's no secret that this new media communication has transformed the way people engage within organizations. In this chapter, we look at global trends and discuss key principles to launch social media programmes internally and overcome hurdles in implementing solutions.

As companies realize the need for enhancing everyday *communications* and constantly innovate to deploy new employee engagement tools, social media is becoming a preferred medium for sharing knowledge and experiences, hence building long-term relationships. In India, with a tracked number of close to 80 million people online, social media is undoubtedly growing in leaps and bounds.

It is estimated that India will touch 45 million social media users by 2012 (Neilsen, 2011). Also Indians today, according to Neilsen's social media usage report, spend more time on networking sites instead of personal email. Other sign of the growing influence of social media in India is Facebook's recent takeover from Orkut as the most popular social networking site.

A report on internal communications (Stromberg Consulting, 2006) shows how true the statement is. The world is surely changing with information as a tool for influence, democracy, and engagement. The trends point to another interesting phenomenon—the rise of personalization. The need to have differentiated, unique content served to your desktop.

The sea change in internal communications is quite evident. From a command-control and formal-directive mechanism, it is today about inclusion and two-way transmission of meaning. There is greater emphasis on engagement and conversation. The options available for communicators have exponentially expanded. The shift towards new media also has another reason—'people tend to trust their peers more than authority figures', says Edelman Trust Barometer (2010b)—putting the employee in the front seat in comparison to the organization's leadership. The Towers Perrin/ IABC 'Future Trends' Study (2002) indicated a greater need for using new media for connecting people.

So who is using social media? According to Edelman's employee communication study (2006), roughly one-third of leading organizations use blogs, and of these, one-third are aimed exclusively at internal audiences. The use of podcasts and wiki technology are gaining popularity. Just look at these mind-boggling statistics for some indication. The number of blogs globally has grown from six million to more than 75.2 million as on May 2007; 10.2 posts every second of every day. The number of podcasts hosted on the internet has surpassed the number of radio stations worldwide. Wikipedia, a public internet-based encyclopaedia launched in 2001 that allows users to create and edit content, has 1.4 million entries in English, more than 10 times that of the *Encyclopaedia Britannica*.

The advantages of social media for internal communications are evident.

From internal expertise and information sharing to perceived openness and collaboration, from accountability and speed to engagement and experimentation—communication is top priority.

Social Media as a channel still has a long way to go before getting completely understood and integrated into internal communications plans. The factors impeding good integration are unclear objectives, lack of understanding, myths, poor practices, and attitudes. Before one can appreciate the new tool, it is critical to ask some pertinent questions on its mission, usage, audience, and expected results.

To begin, internal communications practitioners can make quick hits by solving employees' basic issues of information overload and personalization. But for larger success, internal buy-in from senior leadership on the benefits (which are many—accountability, transparency, trust, engagement) and measurements of the medium is critical.

Practitioners keen to arrive at a concrete new media plan for internal communications can show results with easy-to-manage tools and applications.

How to Start Your Social Media Journey Internally

Many heads better than one: Can you wiki your internal documentation? With this new collaboration tool, you will witness a new-found passion for sharing and integration among your employees.

Leveraging internal expertise: Each employee has unique talents and expertise and you can help harness it for the organization. By connecting experts and channelling a discussion, the time for information access is reduced dramatically. They say we are separated from each other by six degrees of separation. Make those six degrees closer than your employees can think.

Constant beta-testing with your best critics: How often have you wished you got critical feedback to improve your products and services and did not know whom to turn to? Test it on your employees and you will be amazed at the power of insight which comes from them. Today, organizations believe in the power of crowds to fine-tune mission critical applications meant for mass markets. Good examples are Google and Yahoo.

The power of citizen journalism: With new media, the press is no longer the one who creates or brings news first. It can be your employee who blogs, is on social networking sites, and listens to podcasts and has an opinion. Are you aware of where your employees are? Research has shown that a large chunk of their time in office as well is spent on networking sites and gathering content. There is a boom in social networking sites not just abroad but also in India. With international social networking sites such as Facebook, Orkut, MySpace becoming a part of the daily routine for the 38.5 million internet users in India, the Indian social networking sites have a tough task. Reliance ADA group's Bigadda.com, Yaari.com, portal Ibobo.com, Fropper.com, and many others are ready for battle. The internet user base is estimated to grow to 100 million by 2007–2008 (Internet and Mobile Association of India, 2005). It is estimated that 10 per cent of the present internet audience is active on social networking portals, which is close to 4 million users today. Therefore, can you make your employees advocates of your brand by understanding their needs?

Monitor the web: Search Technorati and other leading internet think-tanks for subjects and mentions of your organization. Identify the appropriate channels and share the internal strategy with stakeholders.

Build policies: Institute policies for electronic media usage before the media overrun your organization. It can be a good idea to wiki the policies—IBM arrived at their policies with the help of employees.

Start a conversation: Replace email with an internal blog and get the conversation started. Engage communities of practice on the intranet and offline. Wiki your intranet pages as test case. Make employees accountable for content. Have measurement mechanisms like page rating and popular expert pages.

The Absorb–Adapt–Apply Model for Social Media Adoption

Here is a simple template to chalk out a quick social media plan.

To leverage social media for your organization internally, you can use the following guidelines:

ABSORB
- **What are your goals?** (engagement, awareness, education, leads, etc.)
- **Who is your audience?** (what interests them, how are they currently finding us, how social media savvy are they, which channels are they on)

Table 10.1 Absorb–Adapt–Apply Model for Social Media Adoption

Task	Outcome	Action	Deadline	Review	Progress
Introspection					
Learning					
Strategy					
Networking					
Channels					
Follow-ups					

Source: Verghese (2007).

ADAPT

- **Match content, media and, audience** (what content do you want to share, timing, location, how do they prefer to receive it)
- **Promotion** (search, word of mouth, viral marketing, links)

APPLY

- **Governance and policy** (define members, communities, regulating comments, etc.)
- **Measurement** (how will you measure success, visibility, engagement, content—trackbacks, comments, visits, leads, etc.)
- **Review and improvement** (conduct pilot, update plan, keep fine tuning).

According to an IABC report (2009), over 79 per cent of global companies leverage social media internally to improve productivity and engagement. India, however, still lags behind when it comes to adoption.

To put it mildly, we are still 'scratching the surface'. After speaking with various corporate internal communications practitioners from a spectrum of industries, I am convinced that 'getting started' isn't the issue; it's about getting it right.

From an internal communication perspective, adoption is quite nascent, even in technology firms considered to be leaders in embracing new media. Still, the intent is there. An India-based social media study ranks 'engaging employees with social media' on the list after customers and media—a good indicator of how we are shaping up (Blogworks, 2009).

Seemingly, most social media initiatives within organizations in India are 'wants' rather than 'needs'. Many companies have met with resistance and waning interest since programmes are top-down driven—usually coming from a leader wanting to connect with employees on a blog or an overzealous HR professional trying out a new tool he/she heard about at a conference. Few firms have reached a maturity where a well-defined social media strategy guides how leaders, employees, and internal communities connect for improved collaboration, better engagement, and enhanced productivity.

Challenges in Adoption

Among the reasons why social media adoption is still nascent in India are:

- a lack of understanding and business clarity;
- security concerns;
- sustaining interest overtime;
- information moderation norms;
- the inability to decode cultural nuances.

Poor Understanding of the Medium

Social media is understood in India as a fad, associated with a set of tools that can generate 'buzz', help keep up with the Joneses, make tangible progress at a minimal budget and as a way to build an 'online' presence. Furthermore, employees aren't aware of how to leverage the tools and consider external channels such as Facebook, LinkedIn, and Twitter.

Organizations fail to step back and map their goals as to how social media can be tapped. Often it's seen as 'IT-driven' with only tech-savvy employees using the non-mainstream channel.

Clarity and Purpose

Social media practices often don't have a clear owner within organizations. Mostly there is a team formed from IT, Leadership,

Legal, HR, and Communications who converge to create guidelines and implement solutions. The purpose of social media can often be mistaken for 'quick-wins' that will make teams look good, have a cool quotient, and demonstrate two-way engagement. This approach is usually met with scepticism from employees, surprised to see the company releasing control to enable social media.

Security and Connectivity

Security is another drawback to social media integration, especially with 96 per cent of Indian firms' decision-makers prohibiting the use of these tools in the workplace (Singh, 2010). For example, a global financial services company in India deactivated universal serial bus (USB) ports, prevented access to websites, and kept a strict vigil on employees with video cameras for fraud prevention. Such restrictions only stifled employees' interest to collaborate and made them feel insecure. Letting go of the 'command and control' model is crucial for India to fully realize the potential of social media.

Issues of Trust and Transparency

'If you build it, they will come.' Not so with social media adoption in India. You may have the best infrastructure and invite your employees to participate, but if the culture within isn't open to criticism and feedback, you are going to run into issues. If you have a robust social media system in place but your IT policies block freedom of expression and access to websites, then you will end up with disengaged employees.

If leaders don't see value in social media or label it a 'productivity buster', employees understandably will stay away. Without a clear understanding of the medium, companies will continue to baulk at the idea of setting up discussion forums or allowing comments on blogs defeating the purpose of social media!

Lack of Resources

The lack of dedicated resources within organizations to oversee social media integration adds to the problems. Mostly, it's introduced as a knee-jerk reaction to 'situations'. For example, a global IT services firm with offices in India recently got a wake-up call when 'attacked' on job portal forums and sites like www.glassdoor.com for alleged poor work practices. Ignoring the issue meant eroding the value of the brand. To mitigate this 'risk', the firm instructed employees to post 'positive' messages on the forums. Unfortunately this approach backfired due to the lack of credibility, inconsistent messaging, and the inability to address stakeholders' expectations about the power of social media.

Culture and Sensitivities

Companies choosing to adopt social media need to be aware of the cultural sensitivities that may come along with it. In Indian organizations, hierarchy is respected and unless employees see their leaders participating in or prescribing the medium, they may not think social media is worth the effort.

The generation gap also plays a pivotal role when it comes to channel preferences inside of companies. Other barriers to adopting social media include 'fear' of saying something wrong and being viewed as 'ignorant' among peers. One large Indian conglomerate ran into problems when they found that employees in southern India didn't even know what a blog or wiki looked like! As a result, they changed their strategy by focusing on education to achieve buy-in.

Measurement and ROI

This is still a fuzzy subject due to a lack of understanding and approach. Therefore, measurement is related to looking at usage data (hits, page views, number of comments) while organizations are still grappling with how to demonstrate ROI on social media investment.

Best Practices in India

Most benefits of social media are understood to be short term such as information sharing, faster access to experts, and speed of response. In the long term, fructifying ideas and innovation that emerge from discussions and conversations are considered forward thinking. Organizations are also aware of how online reputation can be fostered and crisis averted though an in-depth knowledge of social media.

As the impact and understanding of social media continue to grow, a handful of organizations are now seizing the opportunities. For example, Bharti (Airtel), a leading telecom organization with over 20,000 employees, switched to an SMS-based intranet based on an IBM tool called me-tize. The move did away with email, got employees connected, increased productivity, added convenience, and also contributed in a 'green' way (Philip, 2009).

Searches on social media trends in India will lead to examples of how the big IT names—HCL, Infosys, Wipro, Tech Mahindra, and TCS—are online and engaging with customers either with leaders sharing information via Twitter or a group of bloggers connecting with audiences. However, those organizations who have made inroads have invested in crafting a policy—surprisingly only 29 per cent of organizations seem to have a formal policy in place (Bullas, 2010), building a culture of collaboration, empowering

141

users on tools and benefits, and inculcating a habit of leveraging tools irrespective of career levels.

Blogging by leaders within the organization is on the rise as a way to connect and energize staff. These instant communication tools provide a sense of transparency and ownership. Intranets and micro-blogging tools are picking up too with 'off-the-shelf' solutions such as Yammer, Jive, and Chatter popular among companies who are keen to experiment. However, the concern of security issues and safety of internal content on an external network are driving most to create in-house assets with 'packaged' options such as Microsoft's SharePoint. Virtual events and webcasts via Webex as well as user generated content around campaigns are also gaining ground as relevant communication channels.

In the area of intranets, there is a shift towards giving more control and accountability to local communication teams with independent pages 'localized' to connect more closely with employees. Staff are invited to share informal personal information and contribute facts to 'get to know you' pages.

In a leading innovation firm, the social media strategy to connect leaders and provide a platform for employees resulted in healthy conversations taking place internally. The objectives were to build a 'great place to work' atmosphere, up the 'cool' factor, and attract the best talent from the market.

Apart from the corporate intranet, which serves as the central channel for communication and hosts tools such as blogs and wikis, the company also invested in recognizing employees for participating. Some blog contributors were even rewarded with gift vouchers and trophies for their effort.

Measurement via organizational health surveys and engagement studies gave communicators and leaders a fair idea on how social media has impacted culture.

Role of the Internal Communicator in Driving Change

Internal communicators are associated with promoting culture by leveraging social media, demonstrating value, creating processes around IT support, and building guidelines and content moderation. They are expected to monitor, facilitate, coach, and work with managers to get buy-in and time from employees within their teams for content generation and sustaining interest.

They are known to look for opportunities to leverage social media tools, encourage leaders and managers to share content often by pointing to relevant themes from an organizational context and mapping out priorities.

Looking Ahead: Strategies to Improve Adoption

Those successfully implementing social media have taken the time to absorb the various elements surrounding this phenomenon and create stringent policies and guidelines to protect IP and the organization's image.

To achieve employee buy-in, consider the mix of age groups within the company and explain the rationale and thinking behind why the company is investing in social media internally and what you expect from your staff.

Communicate the dos but stay clear from policing them. These policies should cover what the user can or cannot say in public forums, sites to avoid, and tips on how to avoid putting the company at risk. The message needs to be that social media is a win-win scenario for the company and for the employee.

It is important to have quick wins. These include arriving at a base document, auditing the talent within, starting a conversation, and then involving employees. My recommendation is that organizations begin with something non-controversial—such as health and wellness, sports (for example, cricket) or work–life balance. Get employees to converse, release control gradually, observe how they interact, and pick insights that you can bring to other forums where you can leverage social connections. Whether you create digital stories on these topics or run a contest to get user generated content, the possibilities are endless.

To groom a pool of social media champions, find employees who are interested in contributing to the social media space either as a content provider, moderator, or a guide. Tap into this pool of media enthusiasts and coach them with bite-sized chunks of messages.

Overall, I see a bright future for social media penetration in India. To move forward, there are some issues that need addressing first:

1. **Social media ROI**
   To measure the actual ROI, it is important to match it to the appropriate objective and result. For example, if the objective is to create a culture of knowledge sharing, then the only tangible way to measure it is by putting a number against transactions, improvement in organizational knowledge, and learning gained.

2. **'Readiness' factor**
   One aspect which most organizations haven't figured out yet is using social media in crisis communications—internally and externally. Right now it's a scramble to get messages out with the help of PR agencies but it's time that communicators realize that 'speed' and 'honesty' are the drivers when it comes to overcoming online reputational concerns.

3. **Know your employees**
   Without understanding user aspirations and needs, social media penetration within organizations may take longer. It helps to conduct an audit of all the social media skills your staff has and leverage them on sites they are on.

4. Internal communicators as social media coaches

I believe that internal communicators must be experts at social media to be acknowledged as partners in this process of transformation. Why would a leader or an associate listen to you if you haven't blogged or know how to start one? How can you be credible if you are unaware of recent trends from industry leaders?

In short, for companies to successfully integrate social media into their internal communications, they need to look inward and address cultural differences, have a plan, be open to accept and acknowledge feedback and criticism, build and leverage robust enterprise-wide systems, and empower employees to experiment.

WORKSHOP

Let us examine the three part AIM framework and see how it works in a situation.

Situation: Your organization wants to launch a company Facebook page. This is the first such social media initiative and the internal communications manager has been assigned with the task of recommending a strategy and plan. What are the steps that the person needs to take to get it right? What pointers will you give to ensure the launch is successful and the page reflects the organization's brand image?

Intervention:

Before you begin, what can be potential questions you can ask the team?

Here are some:

- What does the organization want to achieve with its online/social media presence?
- What are the objectives of the Facebook page?

- Who else in the competitor set or in the local market are active on social media sites?
- What are some of the best practices and learning from their interventions?
- What is the current mindset about social media among leaders and staff?
- Which sites is your staff mostly on?
- Do you have a social media policy in place?

Alignment: *Getting everyone on the same page* for organizational momentum

Run a survey to gauge which sites people are on. Craft a basic social media policy and have all staff build in content based on their experiences and knowledge. Publish a common understanding of what social media means to the organization.

Inclusiveness: *Involving all stakeholders* for a sustainable and consistent experience

Form a core team of social media enthusiasts. Invite staff to test a beta site or a private page before you go live. Have direct control and empower moderators to pull out content that isn't in line with the company's goals. Know that there can be cases (negative comments, bad press, etc.) which can cause panic among moderators—so prepare them in advance.

Get leaders to join the site first and post messages. Avoid launching till you have enough content on the page as well as clear directions for people to interact. Have Gen Y staff train leaders on social media best practices.

Measurement: *Learning from metrics* and making progress from feedback

Prepare a set of scenarios that this core team of moderators may encounter. Help them to think of potential solutions and scenarios. Develop key messages for them to use and share. Think of a long-term plan for content updates and refreshes. Keep reporting our metrics from the site—usage rates, key milestones, top themes, and comments, etc. Collate an ROI from the site—investments made vs positive sentiments received or something similar.

Role of Internal Communicators in Adopting Social Media

Planning to get your organization on the social media map? There are factors that I learnt along the way, which are needed to get completely immersed. Read more about the dos and don'ts of kick-starting your firm's social media communication. Understand also how you can leverage internal communication context and content.

The power of social networking sites can't be ignored and communicators may be worried if your stakeholders are being actively engaged on them. If your organization believes that social media is meant only for the marketing or PR department to handle, they may be missing a great opportunity to maximize the power of your employees and internal communication.

I believe the boundary between the external world and the internal environment is blurring rapidly. Internal communicators who spot this opportunity can maximize the value social media offers. Extending an organization's reach is today an avenue for collaboration between internal communication and external media teams.

If you are, for instance, starting out on a social media campaign, here are some ideas to translate the great work you do internally to feature as your organization's effort to hire, engage, and collaborate with their stakeholders.

Study the scope and environment: You may not be the first to get on any of the well-known social networking sites such as Facebook, LinkedIn, or MySpace. That does not take away anything from getting what you want to achieve by starting out now. Understand what others in your field have done in terms of content, engagement, methodology, and monitoring feedback.

Define how your organization can engage: Do you expect the page to be an extension of your website? Is it a channel to provide support for your products or services? Are you hoping to hire the right candidate? Should you be showcasing your culture? Do you believe your customers will share their practices and pain points on your page? Document the precise objectives and measurement criteria. Get a legal point of view—it never hurts to know what can get you in trouble and out of it!

Get an enthusiastic team in place: This is a cross-pollination project—not an individual initiative. Have employees from different departments to play leading roles in the administration, content generation, and maintenance. Some of the best ideas can come from those fresh out of college—since they use this medium the most!

Create a site map before you tackle the content: Are you clear about how the site will look? Are you sharing a lot more than what you bargain for? By getting a buy-in on the structure and outline, you hold the key to the best outcome from your content.

Articulate the rules of engagement: So you expect your prospects to visit your site? Will you allow them to use it for their personal marketing objectives or do you want them to focus on what you have defined? Do you have a set of 'dos and don'ts' called out?

Content matters: Every organization has a lot to share ranging from their culture, values, ethics, policies, their work, client wins, industry awards, employee testimonials, office imagery, and fun events. Choose how you want your organization to be perceived.

Content once published can always be replicated in no time across the web world.

Pilot a site: Having got your site live, you can begin by getting your employees to test drive it first, get feedback, have them as fans, and improvise.

Get leadership to promote it: Nothing works more than the commitment of your senior leaders. Request a senior leader to officially announce the page open, seek participation, and drive traffic.

So now that you have your company's social networking page live, how can you keep it current?

Invest time to brainstorm ideas such as leveraging 'internal writers' to contribute, getting employee profiles, running a contest, having your recent employee fest showcased, or an upcoming event highlighted. Also give the site mind space on your intranet.

Other thoughts to keep in mind while keep your organization's social networking page buzzing:

Be open: You may have feedback which is scathing and embarrassing. Step back and understand the context of the feedback and take action if merited.

Start small: Begin with the basics and evolve as the page takes shape. Remember, social media is about collaboration, and your employees and other stakeholders can help make it robust.

Monitor progress: Understand that having a page on MySpace or Facebook is not the end but a start of the social media journey.

Keep a finger on the pulse and monitor posts, comments, and inputs coming on the page.

CASE STUDY

Your organization is facing an issue with managing expectations of your staff on social media. Most youngsters were posting company related information and internal photographs on their personal accounts. They were writing their own versions of the events that take place in the organization and inviting comments from friends and families. As an internal communicator, what steps will you take to partner with your social media counterpart to overcome this issue and help staff understand their responsibilities?

STUDENT EXERCISE

Your institute wants to use social media to target prospective students but doesn't know how to begin. The leaders who run the institute are from the old school of thought—they prefer to control information and also haven't used social media sites before. How will you guide them to start something and ensure they meet objectives of connecting with the prospective students' community?

CHAPTER 11

Working with Leadership

In the current times, it is not enough anymore for leaders to take decisions among themselves. Employees are seeking inclusion and transparent methods of decision-making. Effective internal communications is the last resort when it comes to reviving flagging morale or addressing a crisis. The internal communicator's role is often expected to bring in varied degrees of balance and specialized stakeholder management skills.

It isn't easy these days being a leader. With trust, confidence levels, and credibility dropping rapidly among employees, leaders face an uphill task in rallying staff, conveying messages, and moving forward towards the organization's goals. This chapter looks at how internal communicators can improve leaders' presence and improve their relationship with stakeholders.

The usual grouse is that leaders don't show up, are not putting value on communication, aren't straightforward, don't listen, and don't take feedback seriously.

Take, for instance, the Confidence in Leadership Index survey (Korn/Ferry, 2010) that shows that Asia-Pacific leaders fared poorly on the statements posed: 'Our leaders are models of ethical business conduct'; and 'Leaders are quick to admit mistakes and accept responsibility'.

Other research reports such as the Edelman Trust Barometer (2010b), an annual global study of opinion leaders, and the Great Place to Work Survey (2010) indicate that trust among CEOs and leaders is eroding. People tend to believe experts and people like them (peers) instead of leaders.

The average age of staffers in India and especially in sunrise industries such as IT is in the 23–25 year old age bracket. They expect leaders to be hands-on, open to feedback, and take direct responsibility for their actions. This workforce questions authority, keenly observes actions, and wants more empowerment in changing elements within their purview.

It is not enough anymore for leaders to take decisions among themselves. Employees are seeking inclusion and transparent methods of decision-making. They aren't convinced if leaders are only visionaries and strategists. They expect them to gain their trust and walk the talk.

Building leadership credibility is also about being available, wearing multiple hats for the varied scenarios that exist within an organization, and from the expectations of the role. To substantiate that point, the Great Place to Work Survey (2010) indicates that two-way communication, managers' competence, and the integrity and reliability of management are keys to employees' viewing the organization as trustworthy.

So What Can Leaders and Internal Communicators Do to Buck the Trend?

Make communication your mantra: Often communication is the last resort when it comes to reviving flagging morale or addressing a crisis. Employees are not only expecting to get clarity on a host of topics such as revenue and growth, but they also want to know what leaders are doing about attrition, engagement, and social responsibility. Their interest is about the honest, transparent practices within the organization, how we treat our people, how leaders listen, and engage with stakeholders.

Be available: At a Great Place to Work (2010) conference, which I attended, most representatives shared how their leaders were approachable via chat shows, email and face-to-face sessions. It seemed like a privilege for employees to meet with their leaders. It shouldn't be. Rather than hear, 'the leader only shows up in a crisis' or 'never seen the leader around', all leaders must be available when your employees want them to be.

Have your voice: Employees appreciate hierarchy but are open to seeing it is as a structure for better governance rather than a platform for manipulating people. As a leader, you are expected to communicate to those you find yourself in front of, be focused on the future, and articulate personal opinions and vision.

Focus on the future: By focusing on the future, you are also setting an expectation for your employees to look ahead at the upside rather than at any current downsides. Cultivate your personal voice so it is valued through periodic internal communication, be it a monthly report, a weekly blog, or a daily tweet.

Align your managers: Research points to your middle managers as key to the success of any initiative or organizational goal. Getting managers to walk the floors is the most effective way to engage and gain trust. Be it a change in policy or a crisis scenario, it is important for leaders to be present to address concerns. In reality, everyone is a leader and your employees must see their immediate supervisors as leaders. However, you must set expectations on what they can approach you with and what they must deal with up front themselves. Every level of the organization needs to add value to the information you are sharing. Hold managers accountable for the communication they do or don't do.

Check in on your organization's health periodically: While the annual engagement survey will give you a sense of how the morale of your organization is, it helps to keep a regular tab via direct feedback mechanisms and by face-to-face connections.

Solve problems directly: Your employees expect to see you taking action on bottlenecks or concerns that impact their lives daily. Hosting a page with all the feedback and the actions you are taking goes a long way in building transparency and trust. Acknowledge if there is a gap, show intent, and talk of the risk

154

of failure. Then address the issue with your honest opinion. Discuss the pros and cons of the issue, air the solution, and seek an amicable resolution.

Tap experts and personalities: Do you have personalities within your organization who are experts and respected? Leverage their support as communication champions and change agents. Work through these personalities to reinforce messages and empower them with information they can use.

Be prepared to be scrutinized and treated as equals: With information freely available and the speed at which it travels, organizations need to understand that leaders can no longer be exempt from public scrutiny. What they do at work and outside will always be questioned and monitored even if it has no direct relevance to the company's business. Be it in their neighbourhoods, the supermarkets they frequent, the clubs they visit, and the schools their children attend.

Manage personal image and morals: We are all well aware of how the Satyam episode eroded trust (*Business Standard*, 2009). I foresee leaders leveraging the services of internal image consultants to reinvent themselves, not just to understand themselves but to better define their images. Personal image audits will come of age. Tiger Woods and his escapades were splashed across the world's media and are a reminder of how corporate leaders need to manage their images, too.

Leaders and social media usage: With the growing importance and power of social media, leaders will have no choice but to embrace this new media or flounder. Today, leaders' adeptness in understanding what employees discuss beyond the work firewall will be a measure of success. Leaders who are yet to get into the social media world will need to quickly upgrade their skills or be lost in the chatter.

Building Leadership Connection

These days, there is increasing awareness of the merits for tangible connections with senior leadership. To create an 'internal' CEO forum for improved connection with employees, it requires clarity and foresight.

In this section, I share insights on launching and consistently managing an internal leadership forum, be it a face-to-face conversation, chat, 'walk the talk' video version, or even a podcast.

You may have different internal communications objectives to have such a forum; either to improve the leader's image or start a dialogue for the leadership to understand the pulse.

Here are some of my recommendations on crafting a suitable programme:

Get Your Purpose Right

Before diving into the logistics of the forum, know the business objective and how you want to measure progress.

- Are you gauging the 'pulse' of the organization?
- Are you breaking hierarchy?
- Do you want to make the leadership visible?
- Is it a structured meeting or an informal chat?
- Is it a 1:1, many-to-one forum?
- What are the key messages you want employees attending and those not attending to take away?

- How much time does the leadership have to spare?
- Are you confident of consistency and continuity?

Another point to remember is to put emphasis on conducting face-to-face sessions if you need to choose between an online version and a direct 'in the face' conversation. Also, if you have your workforce located in one or two locations in the same city, getting them together at one site is better than creating an expensive online set-up.

Planning and Setting Expectations

Announce the objectives ahead of starting the forums. Set expectations on:

- Format (duration, timing, is there involvement of video footage being captured, number of employees per batch, etc.)
- Logistics
- Venue
- Will you serve breakfast or lunch?
- Will the forum be held on a weekday or a weekend?
- What if there are dropouts? Can others join in their place?

Be sure to have a checklist which contains, among other elements, the communication plan, timelines, registration guidelines, reference material, and the CEO's thank you mailer template.

Brand the Forum but Avoid the Pitfalls

Coining a name and designing an innovative direct mailer to invite participants can work wonders for gaining awareness. However, avoid the temptation to take-off on popular TV chat shows. I remember one organization which used an adaptation of

Koffee with Karan—a celebrity talk show in India and it resulted in employees believing that the communication team lacked creativity and wisdom. The focus shifted from learning more about the programme to what was going to come next.

To avoid such a scenario, I would recommend sticking to something distinct, clear, and easy to relate to depending on how 'formal' or 'informal' you believe the forum should be. It could be something as direct as 'Meet the CEO', 'The CEO Breakfast Forum', or 'CEO Connect Session'. While you make events such as these exclusive, it may also result in a backlash from employees who think it is all 'stage managed' and 'propped'. Transparency and directness is what will make such forums impactful.

Measure What You Do

This is easily the forgotten piece of the puzzle. Unless you monitor participation, feedback from employees and regularly improvise, these forums run the risk of dying a natural death. It is vital to measure based on agreed parameters like format, content, delivery, assimilation of messages, and overall image change of leadership. Refer to the *AIM* model of internal communications.

INVOLVE EMPLOYEES

It is important to garner support from employees for such forums to aid in percolating messages via informal networks and also to gauge impact. Considering you may not get all possible views coming in from your surveys, it makes sense to tap into the 'watercooler' conversations.

REPORT OUT WHEN YOU FINISH

This particular element of the event ensures robustness and clarity. Reporting event summaries, which include questions and key themes discussed, internal communications news snippets, photographs on the intranet or portal, updates to the senior leadership, and results of the survey, guide how the event gets branding and improves focus.

As long as you stick to the three key themes of transparency, consistency, and measurement, you are sure to drive successful internal leadership connection forums.

PERSPECTIVE

The internal communicator's role is often expected to bring in varied degrees of balance and specialized stakeholder management skills. While the role allows you access to leaders and confidential information, it is vital to be careful in storing and sharing information. Working with leaders to me has been a learning curve and I am a long way from getting complete control of managing this community.

You need to know when to 'agree to disagree' on issues and have a good sense when to let go. You need to choose your battles carefully. Think about the big picture and don't get carried away by the small stuff.

For example, an HR Lead whom I worked closely with coined a vision statement for the group and wanted me to 'buy-in'. I found the statement convoluted and not adding value to the process of aligning employees. After numerous conversations and discussions on the verbiage of the statement, I realized that a perception began building about me not being 'flexible' and 'partnering' with the team. At that point, I had to step back and take a hard look at how much the vision statement meant for my work. After mulling over it, I decided to go with what the Lead had worked out, although I made it amply clear that it didn't resonate with me and I looked at it as a statement, nothing more. This decision also helped me focus on other pressing issues and avoid ego clashes that may have ruined my relationship with this leader. It taught me a few lessons.

1. No vision statement can save a team from the quality of work it does.
2. No vision statement is worth dying for and putting your relationship on the line.

3. Be careful of perceptions that build up with every transaction you have with stakeholders.
4. Keep egos in check since there are many to manage around you.
5. Be objective and practical.

CASE STUDY

Vinay is a respected business leader for a large division in your organization. As the company grew over the years, he feels there are many reasons for his division to get visibility among staff. He is keen to begin a newsletter and start communicating. However, there are downsides. If his team begins a newsletter it will trigger copycat reactions from other groups, something you want to avoid as an internal communications manager. How will you go about explaining the need for consistency to Vinay as well as giving him guidance on improving his team's visibility?

STUDENT EXERCISE

As an intern for Company Y, you are supposed to interview a leader for an upcoming organizational event and feature in the internal newsletter. How will you go about setting up the interview and conducting it? What will be the questions you will ask the leader?

CHAPTER 12

Messaging and Internal Communications

Messaging is crucial to the success of communications. In this chapter, we address messaging and how to make internal communications effective. Some important aspects of messaging are addressed and explained with examples as to how internal communicators can define the right messages for audiences.

Messaging is crucial to the success of communications. In this chapter we address messaging and how to make internal communications effective. In this chapter, I will address some of the important aspects of messaging and demonstrate with examples how internal communicators can define the right messages for audiences.

Shreya owns the performance management track at a leading IT firm of 7,000 employees and is interested in driving adoption to a recently upgraded system. The system will bring in wide-ranging changes to how performance management is conducted at the organization. It will save lots of money for the company with reduced paperwork, improved efficiency, and transparent processes. The leadership team is completely behind the new system and wants to implement it right away. A large percentage of staff belong to Generation Y who prefer direct yet informal communication while the leaders are from the old school of thought—they prefer employees following what they are told to do—no questions asked.

Shreya is in a fix. She takes a quick poll among staff and finds that employees lack information, context, and interest in the system or the process. To overcome their mindset, she embarks on a large-scale awareness programme that aims to improve adoption. There is one issue—she has already thought of the cartoon strips that will get published to the employees apart from a set of posters to go up on the notice boards. *Without even a thought about the messages or what will be conveyed through these media. Also not considering what will appeal to the audience?*

Messaging is a crucial element of communication and I am struck by how little awareness there is of its value and potential. A message is the smaller denominator of a theme that you want your audience to take away from your communication. It focuses on one specific expression or action that the recipient is expected to understand or take.

For a message to be effectively crafted, it needs to cover the following:

- What is the ask?
- What is the change?
- Whom does it impact?
- What's in it for me?
- How can I participate?
- What do we want our audiences to do? Do now or in the future?
- How will things be different?
- How do we want me to feel?
- What do we want me to think?
- How/what do I pass on the message to someone else who doesn't know?
- What must I not take for granted?
- What must I look forward to?
- Whom can I expect to get more information from?

In this chapter, I will address some of the important aspects of messaging and demonstrate with examples how internal communicators can define the right messages for audiences.

Messaging aims to summarize all the important and essential features and benefits of your product, service, idea, or offering in a cohesive, coherent manner. It helps distil your ideas into agreed sharable content while allowing better control over communicators, channels, content, and distribution.

According to research studies, information retention levels for traditional communications media can differ quite substantially. The sole use of statistics in a presentation can lead to a retention rate of around 5–10 per cent at best. If you couple the statistics with a bit of storytelling, you can increase the retention rate to around 25–30 per cent. Therefore, a message which tells a story is much more easily understood than one which is plain Jane.

How Can I Define a Message?

To get started, it helps to begin with the basics. Think about the following:

- What are you offering? (Define the offering.)
- What the benefits? What is the change?
- Who is the target audience?
- How is it unique?
- How can your target gain from the offerings?
- How can they receive it?
- How can they contribute?
- How can they give feedback?
- How can they reach the right people?

Here is a situation and the possible messages that can go along with it:

- A few employees fell ill after consuming lunch served in the cafeteria.
- The employees were immediately shifted to a leading city hospital for treatment.
- The food served during lunch has been sent to a nearby lab for independent testing for any contamination.
- We aren't sure of the cause as yet.
- Employees are concerned and have stopped eating lunch at the cafeteria.
- News is spreading on the intranet discussion forums.
- Leaders are unclear how to communicate.
- You need to report out soon to avoid speculation and gossip ruining your credibility.

Here are messages you can construct to convey the situation and the organization's actions:

Key Message 1	Key Message 2	Key Message 3
There are confirmed reports of five employees falling ill after consuming lunch in the cafeteria.	This incident is unprecedented. We are concerned about our employees' health and the impacted employees are under medical care at the city's leading hospital.	We are conducting tests on food served during that meal. We have temporarily stopped service from the vendor until the test results come in. In the meantime, please reach out to your managers or the HR dept. for any other concerns you have.

To ensure you have all stakeholders aligned on your messages, it is useful to prepare a map similar to the one below:

SITUATION

A few employees receive a hoax message that is possibly an attempt to misinform or to inject a virus into the systems.

There is panic amongst employees since the message indicates a possible lay-off in the near future.

The organization's leadership needs to put out a communication that quells the concerns yet keep employee posted on developments.

Here is a shot at how it can get drafted:

165

Table 12.1 Messages Matrix

Goals	Message	Audience	Vehicles	Measurement
To keep employees informed of the real picture	We are aware of an attempt to create confusion among employees of a lay-off. Our primary investigation reveals that the message may have reached 50 per cent of our employees. It may be a virus that damages our systems if forwarded.	Senior leaders, board	Face-to-face conversations	Coverage of teams by leaders
To involve and engage employees in the solution	We are aware of a hoax message that has reached a majority of our employees. It is potentially a virus infected email that can damage our internal systems if forwarded. The IT team is investigating the source and we will keep you posted. If you have clarifications on the email, please reach out to your leaders. We urge that you stay focused on our goals. Our organization's growth story is strong and we expect your ongoing support to achieve success as per our strategy.	All employees, intranet	Email, face-to-face conversations	Direct feedback, survey, engagement pulse

Source: Author.

Back to Shreya's case I shared earlier.

Shreya can rally the workforce by engaging them in a way they understand and participate. That means, her message needs to call out one of the following:

1. As a company, we are moving forward and we want you to help us get to our goal of achieving high performance. Therefore, this system is our best foot forward in our quest to reach our destination. Your support is crucial for our success.

2. You own your career and there is no better way than to equip yourself with the right tools and resources to make progress in our organization. This new system provides you all this and more. All you need to do is attend the training sessions, learn the system, and make the most of the opportunities that we offer.

3. Our organization is steeped in values such as transparency and growth, and this system is aligned to who we are as a company. To make your life simpler and faster, this system has taken into account feedback you shared recently to enhance our processes. Make the most of the quicker, leaner, and predictable application to contribute even more to our shared vision and your own success.

CASE STUDY

Now attempt writing up your messages based on the situation below:

- There is civil unrest in the city where your office is located. There is arson and looting on the streets. Your local workforce comprises expatriates and Indians.
- As part of the communication team, put a detailed crisis communication plan and messages document.

Outline a method for immediate action and steps to ensure all employees are taken care of.

STUDENT EXERCISE

Your institute is moving to an online tool of grading students from the current manual process. Identify and help craft the top five messages your institute director can share with staff and students.

Resources

In this section, I have compiled a set of material that will aid your understanding of the role, how you can be successful at interviewing candidates, etc.

Guides and Templates
a) Guide to Seeking Answers before You Begin
From your manager:
- How is the team structured?
- Which are the core responsibilities?
- What are the team's goals for the year?
- Which are the key channels of internal communications and who are the owners?
- What does your everyday job look like?
- Which project can you begin right away on?
- Which are the most pressing issues for the team?
- What are the challenges that stakeholders usually articulate?
- What are the team's measures of success?
- What is your manager's yardstick to measure you?
- What are your manager's expectations from the team?

From your stakeholders:
- Do they know why you were hired?
- Do they have clear idea of what value you can add?
- Do you know what keeps them up at night?
- What is their current impression of the team's work?
- Is there any specific work that they can recollect?
- How can they partner with the team more?

- Do they know the team's objectives and how it aligns to the organization's goals?
- Which is the most pressing issue they would like to resolve?
- How do they measure your impact?
- What do they need to feel well supported?

Questions to ask yourself:
- Have I understood the company's vision?
- Do I know my team's objectives?
- Have I got introduced to all my team members?
- Does my team know my role and strengths?
- Do I know what capabilities others have?
- Do I know my stakeholders?
- Can I define the top priorities of my stakeholders?
- Do I know the challenges they face?
- Can they reach me and vice-versa?
- What are my short-term, mid-term and long-term expectations?
- What does my day look like?
- Have I got a sense of the processes that I need to follow?

b) **Self-evaluation Guide: How do I know if I am suited for an internal communications role?**

On a scale of 1–5 (where one is low and five is high), where would you rank yourself on the following questions.

KNOWLEDGE AND SKILLS

1. I have read and understood what internal communications is and does to make an impact on an organization.
2. I know the skills that are needed to perform to the best of my abilities in the role.
3. I know how internal communications teams are structured within organizations.
4. I know where I can fit in with my skills.

WORKING STYLE

5. I can multitask and am willing to face changes at work.

6. I am comfortable working with leaders on communication.

7. I am confident of explaining a point of view to stakeholders even if it may be a difficult conversation.

EXECUTION

8. I can follow through a plan with concrete actions and measurable outcomes.

9. I know how to use technology for improving communication.

10. I can network, build relationships, and integrate well with different cultures.

YOUR SCORE AND HOW TO READ YOUR EVALUATION

40–50: You are a great fit and can make your career in this function.

30–40: You have the potential and need to be mentored for this function.

20–30: You need to gain knowledge and skills before joining this function.

Below 20: You may not be suited for this function.

c) **Internal Communications Planning Checklist**

Getting ready to communicate? Look up this checklist to be on track:

- Why and what do we need to communicate?
- What is the connection with your company goals and this communication?

- Who is most suited to communicate?
- What can employees do with the information?
- How can they feel connected?
- Do you know what they think currently?
- Are there changes in the organization that will blend with this communication?
- Is there a sustainable story?
- How is it integrated with external communication?

d) **Town Hall Planning Checklist**

If you are crafting a Town Hall plan, here is a checklist that you can go over before diving into the event.

PURPOSE
- Are you gauging the 'pulse' of the organization?
- Are you breaking hierarchy?
- Do you want to make the leadership visible?
- Is it a structured meeting or an informal chat?
- Is it a 1:1, many-to-one forum?
- What are the key messages you want employees attending and those not attending to take away?
- How much time does the leadership have to spare?
- Are you confident of consistency and continuity?

CHANNEL AND FORMAT
Face-to-face sessions or online chat?

Format (duration, timing, is there involvement of video footage being captured, number of employees per batch, etc.)

LOGISTICS
Venue
- Will you serve breakfast or lunch?
- Will the forum be held on a weekday or a weekend?
- What if there are drop outs? Can others join in their place?

Your checklist must also contain:
- The communication plan
- Timelines
- Registration guidelines
- Reference material
- The leader's thank you mailer template

e) **Interviewer's Guide: What to look for while Interviewing an Internal Communicator**
  This template is useful as an internal communication leader who needs to interview candidates for a suitable role.
  - **Personal** (education, interest, hobbies, etc.)
  - **Team** (how does the candidate fit into the current scheme of things, how does the person engage with the team, whom do they look to for insights and learning, whom do they report to, how do they manage work)
  - **Organization** (how are they making an impact on your organization, how do they know if they are doing so)
  - **Career** (expectations, understanding, and awareness of opportunities available)
  - **Industry** (how aware are they of trends and impact)
  - **Learning** (what investment have they taken to grow, what are they doing to continuously learn more, do they have any mentors)
  - **Personal attributes** (how confident are they, is there clarity of thought, what are their impressions on ethics)
  - **Community** (what are they doing to improve things around themselves, in everyday life, what steps have they taken to make a difference)

f) **Promoting Your Team Template**
  While branding teams internally may not be a viable option for the internal communicator to encourage, it does help to share appropriate channels and opportunities for showcasing the team's goals, progress, and members.
  Here are some pointers to help team's building internal visibility:

1. State what their purpose is and where they plan to be. An informal audit on 'perception' vs 'expectation' will set up a benchmark to work on.
2. Start by sharing their team's plans and agenda, key milestones, and measures as well as outcomes.
3. Begin a regular reporting of progress—either monthly or quarterly to update stakeholders.
4. Leverage the internal portal or intranet to share thought leadership articles—those related to industry trends, plans of the team, etc.
5. Be seen as the 'subject matter expert' in their domain—conduct sessions for employees over and above their responsibilities, reach out, and support teams who need intervention.
6. Share best practices/case studies from the team's work—solutions that got others to succeed.
7. Showcase employees and work from the team that showcases its strengths at senior management forums.
8. Publish content from team events, off sites on the team's page (if this is viable).
9. Peer review any process changes so that the word gets around.
10. Include the team's policy and organization-wide change communication as content within the regular company updates.
11. The team's leader can contribute blog posting and create self-help modules on thought leadership, trends, updates (informal tone, with examples from everyday life).
12. Encourage consistent messaging so that stakeholders observe an aligned team and a common agenda.

Interviews with the Author

The following complete transcripts extracted as interviews with corporate communication and internal communications publications globally may provide insights on the changing face of the function in India.

1. **Internal communications in India: The trend that isn't (Murray, 2008)**

How did you get interested in internal communications?
I was always interested in how people behave within organizations and their relation to communication messages and channels. I got an opportunity to work closely on employee communication projects—redesigning and launching a corporate intranet, crafting an internal communications plan—at i-flex solutions (now Oracle Financial Services). That experience further enhanced my understanding of how critical internal communications was to the success of any organization. I undertook reading more and more articles and research documents on this topic and started a blog in this field. Outside of work, I am a visiting faculty at a local B-school in Bangalore where I teach marketing and communication. I also noticed that the level of understanding of internal communications was pretty low among students and working professionals.

What are your goals within the industry?

I hope to be a thought leader and consultant for organizations and serve as a career mentor for students and working professionals. Also, I am keen to support government and NGO bodies, structure their internal communications framework, and measure the success of these plans.

What are the big challenges/opportunities for internal communications over the next few years?

I foresee internal communicators will play strategic roles in defining how organizations engage, adopt, and manage change. That said, it also means educating leaders on effectively using internal communications to improve reach, visibility, and build community. Internal communicators will also need to embrace social media and integrate it within the realm of how communication is done today, considering user generated content is going to be the future. Helping organizations understand that 'command and control' is over but 'involve and engage' is in. In India, internal communications is still very nascent and most communication is still top-down.

If you had to assess the scope of the internal communications business in India, how would you do it?

In India, the scope and scale is defined largely by the business environment and the organization's interest in employee engagement. Most MNCs operating in India leverage the skills and experience of professionals from their global network to introduce best practices in the region. Issues like attrition, stiff competition for the limited talent pool (specifically the IT industry), and engagement are also drivers to champion internal communications.

At this stage, I feel the practice is quite nascent—some organizations prefer a 'one person–fits all' approach, expecting a professional handling PR to also manage internal communications. Sometimes, HR owns it and sometimes the executive office. It is quite rare to have a separate entity by itself that drives internal communications.

How many internal communications practitioners are there in India—vs five years ago, say?

I would think just a handful. In India, the expectation is to manage more with the limited set of professionals and most often, professionals who do not have the experience or interest are saddled with the responsibility of internal communications. Very few professionals are keen to focus in this specific domain due to a lack of visibility it provides for the individual—also organizations believe it is a skill which anyone can have without investing time and effort.

There is more emphasis in this skill but unfortunately, it is not taught as a separate subject in institutions in the country. At best, it is combined under a larger marketing and communications module.

What are the most urgent tasks of internal communicators in companies in India?

The focus is on building executive presence, cascading internal messages, championing internal campaigns and events. A limited amount of time is spent on strategic thinking and planning, creating messages and standards, improving employee engagement and measuring success.

How will the internal communications scene change over the next year, the next five years?

I see a shift in thinking in recent times to understand the impact of Web 2.0. More and more organizations are conscious of the implications of internal communications on their staff. There is an inclination to knowledge share and learn from best practices.

In the next five years, there will be an increase in the demand for specialists in internal communications, more organizations seeking strategic consulting in this space, and more interest in leveraging social media tools.

Are there opportunities for expats from Europe or the US to come to India to lend their expertise?
In fact, I think it may be the other way around! India and China are top of mind for the world currently and the scenarios in these nations will serve as case studies for global organizations expanding east or in other merging regions. Indian and Chinese communication professionals are being actively sought to understand how internal communications works. Best practices from Europe and the US are cases for reference in India already—some organizations like Accenture, Nokia, BT, IBM are role models for others to emulate in this domain, more from the processes and integration perspectives.

2. Seven skills you need for Internal Communications (Part 1) (Tibaijuka, 2011)

What are the requisites for a career in internal communications?
Usually companies in India do not really select based on any specific requirements when it comes to internal communications—the reason being that this is a nascent subject in this part of the globe and there aren't too many people in the industry who can truly work in this domain. That said, they expect the person to be coming in from a communications background—be it in advertising, PR,

direct marketing, journalism, etc. You also need to have a good grasp of English, have excellent writing skills, leadership abilities, spot opportunities for communication, a dash of enthusiasm, lots of creative ideas, and passion to take up what comes your way.

You will be asked to interface with internal clients and leadership and that requires you to be on your feet, juggling multiple responsibilities, crafting messages, understanding your audiences, planning, designing, communicating, and measuring what you send out.

Today, internal communications offers a wide spectrum of opportunities such as new media, crisis management, event planning, and community building, which at times overlap and even exceed the ambit of public relations. Internal communications is best understood by learning theory, concepts in communication, organizational behaviour, communication planning, and measurement.

Which are the major companies that hire people in this regard?
Most MNCs have a dedicated team that manages internal communications but there is a great deal of awareness among Indian organizations today as well when it comes to this critical domain. Usually, the corporate communication or the marketing and communication team will have individuals who manage internal communications as a separate portfolio or as part of their extended scope. Smaller organizations expect you to do more than just internal communications while larger ones will have you sufficiently occupied managing only internal communications!

And how do I approach companies?
Most of these jobs are never advertised. They are mainly through referrals and therefore it makes it tougher to get to know of these

opportunities. My recommendation to you will be to read up and learn as much as you can about the subject. Then, look up and enrol on blogs and online business community networks which promote or talk of internal communications to get more insight into trends and recent developments.

3. Communicating Bad News Internally

Extract from Q&A submitted to Simply Communicate (www. simply-communicate.com)

> 1. **How managers can effectively handle redundancies— is there any 'good' way to tell people they're losing their jobs?**

I believe being consistent, honest, and direct helps to successfully manage such conversations. It matters how these messages are told more than what we articulate. The best way to say it is by setting context (business demand reducing, revenue not matching with expectation, need to be leaner, etc.) and delivering the rationale on why it affects them. The manager must prepare for all possible questions that may arise during the course of the conversation. These messages are best told face-to-face. There are cultural sensitivities which communicators also need to be aware of. In India, job security is top of mind as stated by many research findings. The social stigma of being 'let go' is tougher to handle. My recommendation is that organizations should conduct these conversations with respect and dignity. They must also aim to keep the lines of communication open even after they are exited, leveraging alumni networks, social forums, career newsletters, blogs, etc.

I am aware of some organizations that release employees 'under the radar' and in small batches to avoid media glare. They may meet their short-term goals but in a socially networked world, word spreads around sooner than we can blink. I think such companies stand to lose more than those who are transparent about their actions and process for elimination.

2. How much emotion should bosses show—or should they take a traditionally stoic approach when communicating the bad news?

Addressing reductions in workforce is a serious affair. The message must be delivered business-like but the manager must be convinced first of the organization's decision and why the person involved is being impacted. Otherwise, it may sound hollow to the impacted individual.

3. How well does management consider the consequences of laying people off (for example, the attitudes/morale of those 'left standing' so to speak, who is left to fill the gaps in slowly dwindling departments, and how the company will perform if key people are no longer working there)?

Management which involves employees in such decisions can be sure of retaining motivated staff in the long run. If they call out the criteria, the thinking behind the decision, and outline the organization's next steps and future, I believe they can honestly request employees to focus on what they do best. There may be some doubts on the minds of employees but answering questions in open forums can alleviate any concerns. Management should lead by example, taking pay-cuts if needed, giving up perks, working more hours, and spending time with employees to demonstrate their commitment. Nothing saps a workforce more than knowing the 'senior management' is still enjoying the luxuries while the going is tough.

> 4. **What kind of resources/information can management make available to employees who might have questions about the inevitable changes that will be occurring following any redundancies/ restructuring? How can managers alleviate employees' fears about the possibility of being next on the list of lay-offs?**

A set of FAQs are a must in such scenarios. These questions should ideally cover elements of the changes such as new organizational chart, vision for the teams, focus areas, ways to contribute professionally for the organization (learning new skills, improving efficiencies, reducing travel, cost and expenditure, innovating on the job, sharing ideas for new business). Connecting employees with outplacement agencies and employee assistance programmes are added benefits that they will value.

Alleviating fears of being on the next 'list' is easier said than done, since employees will only tend to hear what they want to hear. The rumour mills also tend to cloud their thinking. Managers must own responsibility, be available, listen intently, and help employees cope with change.

Questionnaire used to seek inputs from India leaders on internal communications (refer Chapter 5)

- What are the range and expectations of internal communications activities in your organization?
- How is the role of internal communicators changing? How has it evolved over the years?

- What are the challenges internal communicators faces today? Do you feel with business moving beyond the borders and spreading across geographies, internal communicators need to think differently?
- What are the main challenges that you find in dealing with new media (blogs, wiki, podcasts, etc.)?
- In India, has the entry of many large players changed your perspective from talent retention and employee development perspectives?
- Have you used internal communications to manage a crisis in your organization? If yes, please share with us some details.
- Internal communications is more than just passing on messages to employees from the management or vice versa. How difficult is getting a buy-in to internal communications in your organization and what recommendations do you have to overcome hurdles?
- Does your organization hire the services of an external agency supporting internal communications? What are the main attributes that you look for in an agency before hiring one? Also what role do they play and do you think their contribution helps improve internal communications?

References

Bajaj, Gita (2008). 'Tasty Bites Eatable Ltd. (TBEL) Management Case', *Vikalpa*, Vol. 33, No. 3, July–September, pp. 99–109.

Blogworks (2009). 'India Social Media Survey—Brand and Corporates', Edition 1. Available at http://www.slideshare.net/rajeshlalwani/india-social-media-survey-edition-1-by-exchange4mediacom-and-blogworksin-sampler?type=powerpoint (downloaded on 1 May 2010).

Buckingham, Marcus and Coffman, Curt (1999). *First, Break All The Rules: What The World's Greatest Managers Do Differently*. New York: Simon & Schuster.

Bullas, Jeff (2010). 'Only 29% Of Companies Have A Social Media Policy: Is Your Company At Risk?' Available at http://www.jeffbullas.com/2010/02/15/only-29-of-companies-have-a-social-media-policy-is-your-company-at-risk/

Business Standard (2009). 'Slowdown, Satyam Erode Trust in Business: Survey'. Available at http://www.business-standard.com/india/news/slowdown-satyam-erode-trust-in-business-survey/00/06/348349/ (downloaded on 5 July 2011).

Business Standard Reporter (2009). 'SBI Launches Citizen SBI—Fresh HR Initiative', 2 September, Mumbai.

Business World (2007). 'Best Companies to Work for in India'. Available at http://businesstoday.intoday.in/story/the-best-companies-to-work-for-in-india/0/822.html (downloaded on 16 February 2010).

Corporate Leadership Council (2004). 'Driving Performance and Retention Through Employee Engagement'. Available at https://clc.executiveboard.com/Public/Default.aspx (downloaded on 23 March 2012).

Deloitte (2008). 'It's 2008: Do You Know Where Your Talent Is?' A Deloitte Research Study. Available at www.deloitte.com/.../UK_Consulting_TalenMgtResearchReport.pdf

Edelman (2006). 'New Frontiers in Employees Communications'. Edelman Change and Employee Engagement and PeopleMetrics. Available at https://www.edelman.com

Edelman (2010a). '2010: Trends in Organizational (Internal) Communications/ Employee Engagement'.

——— (2010b). 'Annual Global Opinion Leaders Study, Edelman Trust Barometer, 2010'. Available at http://www.edelman.com/trust/2010/ (downloaded on 3 February 2010).

English, Laurel (2005). 'Tying Employee Communications to Organizational Value: In Search of the "Missing Links"', Thesis. Syracuse University. Available at http://www.english-communications.com/downloads/capstone.pdf

European Federation of Internal Communication Association (2009). 'Internal Communications across Europe III'. Available at www.feieo.com/media/ FEIEADelphiStudy 2009.pdf (downloaded on 10 April 2012).

Frauenheim, Ed (2005). 'HCL Technologies', Workforce Management, Vol. 87, No. 17, pp. 25–25.

Great Place to Work Survey (2010). '2011 India's Best Companies to Work For'. Available at http://www.greatplacetowork.net/best-companies/africa-asia-and-oceania/india/indias-best-companies-to-work-for (downloaded on 5 February 2011).

HCL Comnet (2005). 'HCL Comnet Launches a Unique Employee Communication Initiative'. Available at www.hclcomnet.co.in/images/news.../Comnet_radio_press_note.pdf (downloaded on 25 December 2011).

Hewitt Associates (2007). 'Hewitt Announces Best Employers in Asia 2007'. Available at www.hewitt.com (downloaded on 16 February 2010).

IABC (2005). 'Best Practices in Employee Communication: A Study of Global Challenges and Approaches'. Available at http://discovery.iabc.com/view. php?cid=56 (downloaded on 23 March 2012).

——— (2009). 'Employee Engagement Survey', IABC Research Foundation and Buck Consultants. Available at http://www.iabc.com/researchfoundation/ pdf/EmployeeEngagement.pdf (downloaded on 5 April 2010).

Infosys (2007). 'Infosys Intranet Named among "World's 10 Best Intranets" by Nielsen Norman Group'. Available at http://www.infosys.com/newsroom/ press-releases/Pages/infosys-world-best-intranets.aspx (downloaded on 2 March 2012).

Insidedge (2006). 'Insidedge Employee Communications 2006 Best Practices Study'. Available at www.insidedge.net/pdf/bestpractices_Insidedge.pdf (downloaded on 23 March 2012).

Internal Communications Hub (2008). 'Keynote profile: Zrinka Lovrencic, Great Place to Work Institute'. Available at http://www.internalcommshub.

com/open/professional/casestudies/lovrencic.shtml (downloaded on 20 March 2012).

——— (2009). 'On the Quest for World-class Internal Communication'. Melcrum Publishing. Available at http://www.internalcommshub.com/open/strategy/casestudies/joalexander.shtml# (downloaded on 2 March 2012).

Internet and Mobile Association of India (2005). 'India FY'07 E-com to Double!' Available at http://www.iamai.in/PCov_Detail.aspx?nid=869&NMonth=12&NYear=2005 (downloaded on 3 June 2010).

JWT (2007). 'Employee Engagement and the New Age KarmaYogi'. Available at http://coffeeanddonutswithjwtplanning.blogspot.com/2007/11/employee-engagement-and-new-age.html (downloaded on 16 February 2010).

Kalla, Hanna (2005). 'Integrated Internal Communication—A Multidisciplinary Perspective'. *Corporate Communications: An International Journal*, Vol. 10, No. 4, pp. 302–14.

Karian and Box (2008). 'IC Survey 2008'. Available at www.karianandbox.com/html/pdfs/icSurvey2008.pdf (downloaded on 20 March 2012).

Kenexa (2007). 'Corporate Social Responsibility Efforts are Recognized by Employees'. Available at http://www.kenexa.com/getattachment/76533599-b86f-4391-8d50-3b8e35286d3f/Corporate-Social-Responsibility-Efforts-Are-Recogn.aspx (downloaded on 16 February 2010).

Korn/Ferry (2010). 'Confidence in Leadership Index Survey'. Available at http://www.kornferry.com/Library/ViewGallery.asp?LanguageID=1&RegionID=262&CID=11600 (downloaded on 3 February 2010).

Koshy, Anish and Yorke, Peter (2002). 'An Intranet by the People for the People', *Intranet Strategist*, October–November.

Melcrum (2004). 'How to Measure Internal Communications'. Melcrum Publishing Ltd. Available at www.melcrum.com (downloaded on 2 March 2012).

——— (2005). 'Workers "in the Know" Are More Motivated'. Available at http://www.internalcommshub.com/open/news/chasurvey.shtml (downloaded on 5 January 2012).

——— (2009). 'Key Benchmark Data for Communicators'. Available at www.melcrum.com

Mercer (2008). 'What's Working Study'. Available at http://www.mercer.com/whatsworking (downloaded on 5 February 2010).

Murray, David (2008). 'Internal comms in India: The Trend that Isn't', Ragan.com. Available at http://www.hrcommunication.com/Main/Articles/Internal_comms_in_India_The_trend_that_isnt__940.aspx (downloaded on 7 May 2009).

REFERENCES

NASSCOM (2009). *The IT-BPO Sector in India, Strategic Review 2002*, Page 5. NASSCOM, Retrieved from www.nasscom.org/sites/default/.../SR_2012_Executive_Summary.pdf

———— (2012). 'Indian IT-BPO: Trends & Insights'. Available at http://www.nasscom.org/knowledge.professionals (downloaded on 1 March 2012).

Neilsen (2011). 'Indians Now Spent More Time On Social Media Sites Than On Personal Email'. Available at http://www.acnielsen.co.in/news/20110509.shtml (downloaded on 2 March 2012).

Philip, Joji (2009). 'Bharti Adopts IBM's HR Technology: Mobile Phone Doubles up as Intranet', *The Economic Times*. Available at http://articles.economictimes.indiatimes.com/2009-11-10/news/28450408_1_jai-menon-bharti-airtel-smses (downloaded on 5 February 2011).

RescueTime (2008). 'Information Overload—Show me the data!' Available at http://blog.rescuetime.com/2008/06/14/information-overload-show-me-the-data/ (downloaded on 20 March 2012).

Shannon, C. E. (1948). 'A Mathematical Theory of Communication', Reprinted with corrections from *The Bell System Technical Journal*, July, October, Vol. 27, pp. 379–423 and 623–56.

Singh, Seema (2010). 'Socialmedia: Indian Offices most Restrictive', Livemint. Available at http://www.livemint.com/2010/03/24221140/Socialmedia-Indian-offices-mo.html (downloaded on 6 April 2011).

Solari Communication (2012). 'The Most Successful Companies Communicate Better'. Available at www.solari.net (downloaded on 2 March 2012).

Stromberg Consulting (2006). 'Macro Trends in Internal Communications'. Available at http://www.internalcommshub.com/open/news/trends.shtml (downloaded on 12 February 2012).

Sudhakar, B. and Patil, Sujit M. (2006). 'Measuring Up Communication World', *International Association of Business Communicators*, September–October. Available at http://www.thefreelibrary.com/Measuring+up%3A+India's+Tata+Chemicals+Ltd.+scores+with+a+comprehensive...-a0150357842

Tibaijuka, Kagem (2011). '7 Skills you need for Internal Communications (Part 1)', PR Vox. Available at http://www.vox-pop.co.uk/2010/04/09/7-skills-you-need-for-internal-communications-part-1/ (downloaded on 3 March 2012).

Towers Perrin/IABC (2002). 'Future Trends Study'. Available at www.ialic.com/research foundation/pdf/cwo203feature2NOAD.pdf (downloaded on 1 March 2012).

Towers Watson (2010). '2009/2010 Communication ROI Study Report: Capitalizing on Effective Communication'. Available at http://www.towers-watson.com/research/670 (downloaded on 2 February 2012).

Verghese, Aniisu (2007). 'The "Triple A" Strategy: Get Started on Your New Media Initiatives'. Available at http://intraskope.wordpress.com/2007/05/28/the-triple-a-new-media-strategy-get-started-on-your-initiatives/

——— (2011). 'State of the Nation: 2011 India Internal Communications Survey'. Available at www.intraskope.wordpress.com (downloaded on 10 February 2012).

Watson Wyatt (2004). 'Insider Communication Key to Improving Bottom Line—November 2003'. Available at http://www.watsonwyatt.com/render.asp?id=12124&catid=2

——— (2005). 'Effective Employee Communication Linked to Stronger Financial Performance—November 2005'. Available at http://www.watsonwyatt.com/render.asp?catid=1&id=15362

——— (2006). 'Connecting Organizational Communication to Financial Performance, Effective Communication: A Leading Indicator of Financial Performance—2005/2006 Communication ROI Study™'. Available at http://www.watsonwyatt.com/research/resrender.asp?id=w-868&page=1 (downloaded on 2 February 2012).

——— (2008a). 'Driving Employee Engagement in a Global Workforce—2007/2008 Global Work Attitudes R. Available at www.watsonwyatt.com/research/pdfs/2007-US-0298.pdf (downloaded on 2 March 2012).

——— (2008b). 'Increasing Employee Engagement: Strategies for Enhancing Business and Individual Performance', *Work Asia Survey*. Available at http://www.watsonwyatt.com/asiapacific/research/docs/WorkAsia_Survey Report_2007-2008.pdf (downloaded on 2 March 2012).

Welch, Mary and Jackson, Paul R. (2007). 'Rethinking Internal Communications: A Stakeholder Approach, Corporate Communications', *An International Journal*, Emerald Group Publishing Limited, Vol. 12, No. 2, pp. 177–98.

Yorke, Peter (2004). *Maximizing the Value of Internal Communication* [PowerPoint slides]. Available at www.iabc.com/education/docs/Peter_Yorke_108.ppt (downloaded on 2 February 2012).

Internal Communications Online Resources
www.iabc.com
www.ragan.com
www.melcrum.com
www.simply-communicate.com
www.intraskope.wordpress.com

Index

About the Author

Aniisu K. Verghese is an internal communication expert with over twelve years of experience in the evolving employee communications, social media, and advertising domains with leading IT, financial services, and consulting organizations in India. He currently serves as the India Internal Communications Lead for a global IT services firm.

In his earlier capacity he managed transformational internal communication assignments with Fidelity, Accenture and i-flex solutions. He helped launch and manage corporate intranets, edit and publish company employee newsletters, coached senior leadership on communication strategy, led internal branding campaigns as well as crafted effective corporate social responsibility communication that improved employee engagement. Aniisu began his career as a brand executive with Leo Burnett, Bangladesh, and Saatchi & Saatchi, India, creatively contributing to the growth of the Nestle, British American Tobacco, BPL, and Tata Tea accounts.

Besides his work, Aniisu blogs India's and Asia's first dialogue on internal communication—Intraskope (www.intraskope.wordpress.com), which has been featured in global publications such as *Melcrum* and *Simply Communicate*.

He is the founder member of the global road safety campaign and the public interest group—Friends for Life (FFL) in India. The World Health Organization invited FFL for an NGO consultative meet in Geneva, Switzerland, in September 2003. Aniisu was the only Indian to attend the session which preceded World Health Day 2004, dedicated to road safety globally. He won a bronze at the 14th Godfrey Philips Bravery Awards (2005) for his work on road safety.

He is a speaker at management forums and recently addressed about 100 global communicators at the 2011 World International Association of Business Communicators, San Diego, US. He conducts internal communications workshops in the region and recently has engaged practitioners at India's first ever internal communication workshop, 'Internal Communications 101: Essentials for Success', at Bangalore.

Aniisu contributes thought leadership articles for management publications such as *simply communicate* and *Melcrum*.

He is also a visiting faculty for leading B-schools in the country and has designed the integrated corporate communications course for St Joseph's College of Business Administration, Bangalore and St Aloysius College, Mangalore. Aniisu has a certificate in Neuro Linguistic Programming and Usability Testing. He has won honours at the 2002 and 2003 League of American Communication Professionals (LACP) Vision Awards and Society of Technical Communications Competitions, Australia Chapter in the employee publication category.

For further information and interaction with the author, go to http://in.linkedin.com/in/aniisu, www.twitter.com/aniisu, http://independent.academin.edu/AniisuKVerghese, www.intraskope.com.